Sailing The Golden Sea

Sailing The Golden Sea

The Adventures Of Two Sunset Sailors

By
Paul Keller

Illustrated by Emily Keller

Portside Publishing
Portland, Oregon

Copyright 1992 by Paul and Emily Keller
All rights reserved
Library of Congress Catalog Number 91-091485
ISBN 0-9631759-0-4

This book may not be reproduced in whole or in part, by mimeograph or any other means, without permission. For information address:
Portside Publishing
9498 S.W. Barbur Blvd., Suite 305
Portland, OR 97219

Dedication:

To Floyd
In Memoriam

Acknowledgments

When I think of all the reasons why this book exists, the foremost must be the encouragement of our many friends who enjoyed my "Dear Friends" letters and responded by saying "Paul, you ought to write a book." First among those was June Flemming, an outdoors person and author who had been my friend for years. Also, Kenneth Waddell, a retired childhood friend and ardent outdoorsman, thought that my book should exist as an inspiration to others who have retired and found they had "nothing to do." Personally, I just wrote it to share the joy I have for living with anyone who would pick it up and read it. But ideas are one thing, results are another. Several wonderful people guided us through the publishing process and Sharon Castlen, a dynamo of efficiency, answered our question, "Now that we have a book, what do we do with it?" But, most of all, Emily, my beloved wife and the illustrator of our book, made all of this possible with her love and companionship, which may be, in the final analysis, what this book is all about.

Paul H. Keller

Portland, Oregon
February 14, 1992

Old age hath yet his honor and his toll;
Death closes all: but something ere the end,
   Some work of noble note, may yet be done,
Not unbecoming men that strove with Gods.
   The lights begin to twinkle from the rocks:
The long day wanes: the slow moon climbs:
   The deep moans round with many voices.
Come my friends,
   "Tis not too late to seek a newer world.
Push off, and sitting well in order smite
   The sounding furrows; for my purpose
holds
   To sail beyond the sunset, and the baths
Of all the western stars, until I die.
   It may be we shall touch the Happy Isles,
And see the great Achilles, whom we knew.
   Tho' much is taken, such abides; and tho'
We are not now that strength which in old days
   Moved earth and heaven; that which we are,
We are; one equal temper of heroic hearts,
   Made weak by time and fate, but strong in
will
   To strive, to seek, to find, and not to yield.

From Ulysses by Alfred Lord Tennyson

Sailing the Golden Sea

Table of Contents

1	Introduction and Coastal Journey	1
2	Cabo San Lucas to the Marquesa Islands	10
3	Society Islands	24
4	Tonga	40
5	New Zealand, North Island	53
6	New Zealand, South Island	70
7	Scotland and Golden Bell	81
8	England, South Coast	89
9	Paris and the Canals	98
10	French Canals II	113
11	Barcelona Winter	128
12	Balearics, Italy and Greece	139
13	The Cyclades to Turkey	153
14	Winter in Turkey	166
15	Cruising Turkey	178
16	Cyprus	189
17	The Aborted Atlantic Crossing	206
18	About Cruising	219

1

Introduction and Coastal Journey

It is a long way from the dusty Nebraska town of Ainsworth to Opua in New Zealand's Bay of Islands. It took me 50 years to make the journey and I learned three things in the doing. The first is don't let your dreams die. The second is if you are in reasonably good health you are never too old to live your dream. And the third is you need a compatible mate. Who said love is just for kids?

In my sixty-fourth year, everything came together. I had the boat to sail the South Pacific, I had the time, having just retired, and I met my dream woman.

Often I think back to my first meeting with Emily with some fear. What if it hadn't happened? Would I be half as happy as I am now? Would I still be living on our boat and touring the world? Such fears always quickly dissolve into a feeling of blissful contentment. It did happen!

It was a sunny winter day in January on Mount Hood in Oregon. I was a week-end ski instructor and the boss said, "You have a private lesson. She's standing over there and wants to improve her speed on cross-country skis." As the lesson progressed I noted a trim figure, a sparkle in her eyes, and an understated skill on skis. I found out she was adventurous, loved to travel, and was well educated. She talked of hiking in Switzerland and trekking to the Mount Everest base camp in Nepal. Here was a woman, I thought, who liked risk, whose horizons were not limited by doubt or uncertainty.

The day was warm and she took off her gloves and asked if I would carry them in my parka pocket. To this day she does not admit that she forgot on purpose to ask me for them when she left. I called her the next day just before lunchtime to ask if I could return them. She suggested that we meet and have a bite together. Of course, this led to further meetings.

Many dates later, I decided that at sixty-four years of age I was smitten. I'd found the companion I wanted to share my dreams with. But would she have me? How would she take to life on a small sailing boat? She was a physician nearing retirement from her teaching job at a major medical university. I would have to lay careful groundwork. I knew her hobby was painting. Sailing with me around the world would give her plenty of

opportunities to put her impressions on canvas. That was one good argument in my favor. I thought my proposal speech to her was persuasive: "How would you like to join me and spend the rest of your life painting while lounging in the sun on the deck in the shade of a tropical island? Imagine the soft strains of Polynesian music floating through the air and the gentle trade winds caressing your cheeks. Clear tropical waters lap softly on the white beaches just off our bow. How does that sound to you?"
"Very tempting," she said.
"Well, I love you. Will you marry me?"
Emily looked at me and smiled. "The sweet old lady from whom I bought this house told me that the wisteria on the back porch would not bloom profusely unless there was love in the house. Well, it is blooming like crazy!"
"Is that a yes?" I asked.
"Something like that," she said.
From that point on we made plans. We talked about what boat life would be like and of her retirement from Oregon Health Sciences University where she was an associate professor of Pediatrics. Timing was discussed and we agreed to be married "somewhere" in the South Pacific as soon as she could complete her academic year in July of 1985 and qualify for her retirement pension. I refused to alter my date for leaving Portland on the first leg of my journey to the South Pacific. It was set for September 22, 1984. I didn't want to risk delaying my dream, or interfering with its beginning.
So, as scheduled, I left Portland on September 22, two weeks after my last class as a lecturer at Portland City College. I had resigned my job as head of the Business and

Economics Department at Warner Pacific College two years earlier and had been lecturing part-time and getting the boat ready for sea.

The gala casting off party at the Harbor One Marina on the Columbia River was attended by many friends and my children. Since it was a week-end, my future bride sailed with me down the Columbia River to Astoria where I would head south to San Francisco, the first portion of my coastal journey.

Two friends accompanied me on a relatively uneventful sail from Astoria, Oregon to the Golden Gate. One became so seasick he was confined to his bunk for the entire trip. The Oregon coast has a reputation for being stormy and it lived up to it during this leg.

We planned for Emily to join me on her vacation in San Francisco and crew for me on the leg to San Diego—with a few stops along the way. I was eagerly anticipating her arrival and her first exposure to life at sea. I was a little apprehensive as she had never sailed on the ocean or spent a night at sea. Would she enjoy it or not? As it was, she would not be tested at this time.

Murphy's Law says that the worst will happen at the worst possible time. It proved to be true for Emily and me as we exited Berkeley Marina for the open waters of San Francisco Bay. The motor died in Golden Fleece just as we swung into the narrow entrance and we were caught in a strong cross wind. I quickly dropped a bow anchor to prevent us from drifting onto the rocks of the breakwater and called the marina on the radio to ask them to send us a tow. Back at the marina, a mechanic we called pronounced the engine unrepairable. The training trip we had planned down the California coast to give Emily her sea legs was converted into a pleasant few days on the estuary in Alameda, while the new engine was installed. As a result, Emily's first night at sea was not in sheltered California waters, but four weeks later aboard Golden Fleece at Cabo San Lucas in Baja California. She met me there and we honeymooned briefly before I departed on the next leg of my journey to the Marquesas Islands.

As a result of the down time for the engine replacement, I had lost my crew of one, namely Emily, for the southerly leg to San Diego. So I obtained the help of a young man in San Francisco who had sailing experience. My first phone call when we reached San Diego was to Emily. She said friends of hers were disappointed by the idea that she was going to be married in Tahiti, the far-off spot we had picked to tie the knot after she was free from her university job.

"Do you want to get married right now?" I asked.

"It would be nice," she said.

"OK, you set a date and I'll fly home," I replied.

She did and I did and everybody was there.

The wedding took place in the parlor of Emily's long-time friends, Neil and Sonia Buist. They had sort of adopted this single woman into their family years earlier, and Emily was the godparent of their middle daughter, Alison. Catriona, and Diana were their other two daughters who, with Alison formed a shining trio of flashing red hair. My children, Tom, with his wife Becky Magee, and Sue, my daughter, with my two grandchildren were also present. Her husband Greg was at work. Many of Emily's friends showed up and each contributed an outstanding pot-luck offering.

Emily and I exchanged vows and I realized as I

stood next to this fine woman that we were far younger than our years. We were embarking on an adventure that is the most exciting and rewarding one of all—the one of the heart seeking "an equal temper" with another. I thought of the marvelous lines from Alfred Lord Tennyson's "Ulysses." They best described us as we promised our love to one another that day:

> "We are not now that strength which in old days
> Moved earth and heaven; that which we are,
> We are; one equal temper of heroic hearts,
> Made weak by time and fate, but strong in will
> To strive, to seek, to find, and not to yield."

After the ceremony, Emily and I celebrated with champagne sipped from centuries-old silver cups handed down in the Buist family from generation to generation and used only on special occasions. After we had eaten, we swirled to a vigorous Scottish reel led by Neil who, deferentially, had not worn his kilt, probably to avoid upstaging me in my simple business suit.

The next day I returned to the boat in San Diego, leaving Emily to explain to her colleagues why her new husband had left the day after the wedding.

In a way I was glad Emily had not been with me when I visited Catalina in Golden Fleece before arriving in San Diego. As a young man, I had fallen in love with Catalina. Music from this fabled isle came to me in far off Ainsworth (middle of nowhere), Nebraska and I had actually seen the island from afar when I was a war worker in Los Angeles in 1941. The coast was closed on December 8, 1941, so I had to wait. I had planned to save my money and go there some day. Now, 43 years later, I approached it in my own boat.

I have never seen so many boats in one place as I saw in that marina at Avalon. We were forced to anchor on a narrow shelf outside and the situation was so precarious that I decided not to take the dinghy ashore. It didn't look as if there was any place to land the dinghy anyway. A huge patch of the lovely island had been grossly scarred by bulldozers just north of the town and this so destroyed the earlier image I had held in my mind that I just wanted to leave. I suppose by now the patch has been covered with ticky-tacky condos, but at least the Casino was still there and apparently unchanged.

Somehow the excursion to Catalina reminded me of an experience I had during World War II. While in the Navy, I had served on a destroyer-escort which went in and out of San Diego Harbor performing coastal missions just after the war ended.

Several times as our ship left the, bay we had to pass through a clutter of sleek sailboats participating in races in the bay. Our skipper had proper respect for sails and always maneuvered to avoid them if possible. One sailboat skipper became incensed and tossed a few expletives our way when we blanketed his wind.

Then was born my hope that someday I would be sailing my own boat on this bay and get a salute from a big navy ship. My moment came four decades later as we left the bay in Golden Fleece. One of my crew members at the time had sailed in Australia and had remarked that when you dipped your flag in that country you always received an answering dip from a vessel regardless of size. But, he said, U.S. Navy vessels are apparently not too observant of this courtesy. So, as a passing vessel, a huge small cruiser, bore down on us, we decided to test the U.S. Navy. As our ships passed, I slowly dipped our flag. For a moment nothing happened, but suddenly a loud "Hey, pop to!" sounded across the water. There was a bit of scurrying on the bridge and their flag slowly descended in acknowledgement of our salute. The honor of the U.S. Navy had been saved by one alert officer who had stirred some quartermasters to action.

Four weeks after we were married, Emily joined me in Cabo San Lucas and we had our brief honeymoon coinciding with Emily's university's Christmas break. Two events stand out from that episode. The entire fleet of cruisers in the bay of Cabo San Lucas "met" daily on a radio network, and, since it was Christmas, a Christmas Party was organized at a local restaurant.

"See how much fun we cruisers have," I said to Emily hoping she would, by now, two days later, have forgotten our wet dinghy trip out to our boat in the driving rain. We shared a memorable incident at the local Cabo San Lucas Christmas parade. Santa appeared in his typical crimson regalia, but he rode in a small boat on a trailer behind a jeep and threw candy out to the children as he passed.

Emily returned to Portland and it was a dramatic moment for me when we said goodbye at the airport. We had hardly begun our honeymoon and yet it would be six months and 5,000 miles of ocean I would travel before we would see each other again.

When I left Portland, I had promised to write to a number of friends and had devised the scheme of writing one substantial letter describing what I had done and seen in the previous two or three months, having it duplicated and having it mailed by my son. The following chapters are those letters. The illustrations are Emily's contribution to our book. They are sketches she made along the way and each one relates to the chapter content. I hope you enjoy our book and that it may serve as an encouragement to others who think that they are "too old" to follow their dreams.

Plotting our course

2

Taiohae Bay, Nuka Hiva
The Marquesas Islands, French Polynesia
March 27, 1985

Dear Friends,

When I left Portland, Oregon and set off down the Columbia River to the sea five months ago, I told many people that I would write. In Cabo San Lucas I wrote a short letter and sent it home to my son, Tom, who is my permanent address in Portland. He agreed to duplicate the letter and send it out to the short list of friends to whom I had promised to write. With the addition of my Ainsworth high school class to the list and a few others along the way,

I have decided to write more carefully, cut down the number of misspellings and typos, and to include more of my adventures. You, my friends, deserve more than the hurried scrap of paper I dashed off in Cabo San Lucas. Each year in January the South Pacific cruisers begin to gather at three major points for the long haul down to the Marquesas Islands, the most easterly of the French Polynesian island groups. January marks the end of the hurricane season and the beginning of the trade winds. This is the longest leg of the "Coconut Milk Run" as this exodus across the South Pacific has been named. From the Marquesas group, the cruisers pass on to the Tuomotus and then the Societies, all a part of French Polynesia. After that, they continue on to the Cook Islands, the kingdom of Tonga, the Fiji Islands, and possibly as far as Samoa. There, at Tonga, Fiji, or Samoa, the cruisers usually go down to New Zealand for the next "bad weather season," probably starting in October or November. This first leg to the Marquesas is awesome and the hurdle that must be overcome if one is to enjoy the delights of Polynesia. San Diego to Nuka Hiva - 2,500 miles; Cabo San Lucas to Nuka Hiva - 2,500 miles; Panama to Nuka Hiva - 3,800 miles.

We, Curt, my crewman, and I were officially in the South Pacific which most romantics consider the dream goal of most men and a surprising number of women. Getting there was perhaps the biggest challenge I've faced in my life. I'd like to say that it was a piece of cake. Well, it was and it wasn't. Those who say that it is easy either have never made a crossing or were extremely lucky in not encountering any storms. They also may have had all sorts of electronic navigational aids that did not fail during the passage. Every crossing is unique and the sailor who does not plan for the worst is likely to experience it. Someone said, "The sea is a demanding mistress." She is also an unforgiving one to those who are careless or incompetent.

That crossing was not my first as I had sailed to Hawaii some years before as a crew member on a friend's sailboat. This was different. On the Hawaiian crossing; my friend was the captain with the responsibility. I was the crew with none. I trusted him to get us there safely. On the crossing to the Marquesas, I was the captain and Curt trusted me to get us there, not to mention that back in Portland my new bride expected me to get there.

How I was looking forward to that moment when my new "crew" would join me for the rest of my life. If I had all the skills and courage necessary, we would make it. If I failed in any critical way, we would be just another boat lost at sea.

My crewman, Curt, was young, strong, willing, anxious to learn and, most of all, did not get seasick. Curt had sailed with me before. He was enthusiastic about sailing and had always been available; he had a job that did not tie him down.

Curt arrived in Cabo San Lucas early in January and we made plans to leave about the first of February. This marks the end of the hurricane season so the timing is significant. The southeasterlies start to flow about then as the Southern Hemisphere moves away from the sun. Cabo San Lucas had little to offer in provisions for a 4,000 mile sailing excursion. La Paz, only a couple of days away by sail on the east coast of Baja California, was a good-sized town, however, and had many fine stores, especially supermarkets. Curt and I decided to shop there as there was still plenty of time left in our sailing "window" for the Marquesas.

An experience at the end of our first day demonstrates the camaraderie of sailboaters where ever they cluster. We sailed into a lovely bay and discovered several anchored boats. On the VHF radio I hailed them with "This is Golden Fleece to the boats in the bay. Is there room for another boat to anchor?" A quick answer came back: "Golden Fleece, this is Tranquility. There sure is, and we are having a pot-luck picnic on the beach this evening. Join us." I had just caught a jackfish so I had a contribution to the picnic. The fish got grilled on someone's barbecue and disappeared during the feast. I never got a bite of it.

In La Paz we anchored in the bay and experienced the "La Paz waltz." A strong tidal current in the bay changes every six hours and anchored boats suddenly switch direction and do a sort of maritime jig. If you are not expecting it, it can be unnerving.

The stores and supermarkets in La Paz lived up to their reputation. Curt and I bought all sorts of things, enough provisions, I thought, to get us to Papeete, Tahiti.

In La Paz, there is a colorful local institution called "the morning VHF Net." All the boats in the harbor get together by radio and exchange gossip, news, information on needed boat parts, and other suggestions and ideas. The VHF Net was started by a woman who had been a cruiser, but who now lived ashore. She satisfied her longing for the sea by creating a daily boat community conversation. It was a useful service, something like an informal party line where each participant could chime in with a contribution, a question, or an observation that might be useful to somebody.

This same woman held a Friday afternoon bash at her apartment. Bring your own bottle. We discovered at the party that there was a meeting of cruisers who were planning the crossing to the Marquesas. The idea was to exchange information that might prove useful to any one of the group. I met Larry and Melba of the boat Endurance. The four of us, Curt included, shared some beer and sailor-talk one afternoon. They suggested that Endurance and Golden Fleece buddy-boat across the Pacific. They couldn't start until they got charts they needed, however.

A couple of hours later they rowed over in their dinghy. A phone call to San Diego had dissipated their concern about charts. They were being sent immediately. That cleared the way for a buddy passage to Nuku Hiva.

I was overjoyed for two reasons. The Endurance was equipped with a Sat Nav—a navigation system that received radio signals from an orbiting satellite enabling a boat operator to calculate his position within two miles at any time. The second reason was that two boats traveling on a parallel course ensure companionship and emergency help if something goes wrong with one of them.

On February 17th, Golden Fleece and Endurance raised anchor and sailed out of Cabo San Lucas for Nuku Hiva in the Marquesas. Needless to say, I was excited, reluctant, and eager to get started. When 1 gave Curt the order to hoist anchor it was like stepping off into the unknown. I was turning my back on safety, comfort, and civilization to set off on a great adventure. It might be a month before we would drop anchor again. What lay ahead? Storms? Calms? Sharks? Accidents? Injuries? It was a sea of uncertainty. Danger was ahead of us, certainly, but also days of unforgettable sailing, a bracing mixture of salt and sun, wind and water—all combining to impart a feeling of total confidence joined with a new measure of humility and gratitude for being alive.

My nagging doubt was about my ability with the sextant. Maybe the system I'd learned of shooting the stars and sun for direction and location just might not work. I had read many sea stories and knew that all captains experienced periods of uncertainty and doubt about their sighting abilities on a voyage. Once they made their initial landfall most of their doubts vanished.

Frankly, I am in awe of the early Polynesians who could navigate long distances without sextants or chronometers, yet infallibly they arrived where they wanted to go after sailing thousands of miles on trackless seas. How did they do it?

In his book, *We, the Navigators*, Dr. David Lewis actually voyaged with one of the last of the great Polynesian navigators. Just for safety, a friend with a sextant in a modern sailboat accompanied them, but he had strict orders not to disclose any navigation information. They sailed from the island of Kauai in Hawaii to Tahiti in a typical native ocean canoe.

Their ancient navigation system consisted of a complete familiarity with the stars—and a thorough knowledge of their environment. Each island, through legend and study, had its "star." Over 150 of these stars were known—so, if a voyager were sailing from Papeete to Kauai he sailed north until the Kauai star was directly overhead, then he sailed west keeping this star overhead. Of course, in a pitching small boat, it was difficult to know precisely where "overhead" was.

Such a situation is where the sailor's intimacy with

the environment comes into play. There are birds who fly out to sea from the island as far as 40 miles to fish each day and return at dusk to roost. Simple mathematics tells an observer that this deduction turns a 10-mile wide island into a 90-mile wide target. The change in direction of the swells, the different color of clouds over land, all contribute to the sailors' identification of their objective. The navigators' uncanny sense of time also enables them to identify the stars and maintain direction.

As the huge rocks of Cabo San Lucas sank into the sea off our stern, the winds were fresh, but not strong and my heart sang with ecstasy. Fresh, mild winds accompanied us for most of our voyage. We maintained radio contact with Endurance every two hours and twice daily we would update our position with the Sat Nav.

I began to take sights on the sun with my instrument and was getting pretty good readings. A few were way off, but I discovered the problem was usually an error in my calculations.

Soon Golden Fleece entered the shipping lanes from the Panama Canal to the west coast of North America and occasionally we sighted three freighters at one time. The direction of the freighters worried us at night. Their lights gave an indication of how they were heading but how close they might be coming to our course was not apparent until a ship was almost on us.

Frequently we contacted them on the VHF radio in order to let them know that we were nearby and asked them if they saw our lights.

One frightening moment, slightly amusing, occurred when it was apparent that a freighter was going to pass between Endurance and Golden Fleece. I had tried repeatedly to contact the freighter on the VHF, without success, and so had Endurance. Suddenly it made a panic stop and then proceeded slowly and sedately, like a buxom lady in tight shoes, between us. I suppose the freighter's crew had mistakenly decided for a moment that the two sets of lights, visible from the freighter's bridge, ours and Endurance's, might be a tug with barge in tow. These were not uncommon in these waters. If the captain had responded on the VHF we could have encouraged him to proceed without stopping.

Many of the freighters are manned by foreign crews and only the captain speaks English as required by international law. The captain was probably asleep and the Korean crew was afraid to wake him. In another encounter, we had a delightful conversation lasting almost a half-hour with a tug captain who contacted us to make sure that we knew about a huge cable stretched between his tug and his tow which was a half-mile astern.

Another incident occurred when we lost Endurance one night. We were in touch on the radio, but couldn't see each other's sails. We both, however, could see a large freighter passing by. Each of us vectored in on it and we were soon in sight again.

By then, several days out from Cabo San Lucas, we had settled down into a daily routine of picking up the flying fish off the decks every morning. Part of the daily pace was the radio contact we made every two hours with Endurance. Larry was always happy to keep us posted on the delectable dishes Melba was cooking on their boat. We enjoyed them vicariously as we boiled another pot of rice or frijoles and opened another can of tuna or corned beef.

We towed a line aft hoping for an occasional fresh

tuna or mahi-mahi, but we just lost a lot of $3.00 lures to bigger fish or sharks.

About the fifth day out, we saw a sail on the horizon and immediately turned on the VHF and spoke to the boat operator. The boat was a Swan 65 on the way to San Francisco and the crew had elected to take one long tack out to the west hoping to curve back in touching the coast at San Diego.

It is exciting to see another sail "way out there."

On February 28th we lost sight of Endurance and never saw her again until we sailed into Taiohae Bay at Nuka Hiva. We maintained contact for a few days on the ham radio, but we sailed slower than they did since we had a shorter waterline. I told them, regretfully, to just go on alone. Now we were on our own!

I agonized over each daily sun shot I made with my sextant. The quick and easy noon sight was not working anymore because the sun was too high in the sky. We were too near the equator. However, several planet and moon shots turned out well. I was aware there was still a huge error between my dead reckoning and my sights. I puzzled over this until I remembered that there was an equatorial current of 20 miles per day. When I factored this into the equations, things came together much more smoothly. Later, I talked to a famous world sailor who told me: "What did you expect? The toughest latitudes known are those near the equator."

During the long nights, with Golden Fleece hissing through the blue water, I often stood on deck touched with salt spray thinking about Emily, how lucky I was, and how much I missed her. And I admit I felt a small apprehension that she might not have the same burning attachment to the sea that I had.

But I refused to borrow trouble. She was my new bride. What a great day it would be when she arrived in Papeete.

Bathing on the high seas in a small boat is accomplished when the opportunity arises. Salt water is the currency at hand and is often used if rain is not handy.

Fresh-water bathing occurs when you are fortunate enough to be caught in a squall with heavy rainfall. You stand in the downpour on deck singing and lathering. If it lasts long enough, you stop up the drains in the cockpit, throw in a little detergent, and all your dirty clothes. It is an exhilarating experience.

We made no attempt to collect drinking water when it rained because we had stored a substantial amount of fresh water in the tanks. Normally this is the first order of business on many cruising boats which do not have large storage capacity.

The days and nights near the equator were warm so we soon grew weary of our clothes and abandoned them. Cooking, of course, was a challenge as the boat was in constant motion. For breakfast we usually had pancakes, oatmeal or French toast when I made bread, and, of course, eggs. We had no refrigeration since only the largest boats have freezers. We tried to be creative with our meals, but what can you do with Spam, corned beef, and tuna?

Eating was more of a challenge than the cooking. The stove was gimbaled and there were clamps to hold the pots on it. But as the boat tossed in the waves, the food on your plate, and often the plate also, went flying. We developed special techniques for defying gravity at meal times. One trick was using a damp towel on the table to stop plates from sliding.

At the end of the day, we enjoyed our cocktail hour. On Golden Fleece we had, for some reason, skimped on stocking the liquor locker when we shopped in La Paz. Two-thirds of the way across the Pacific, we ran out of bottled liquor. Ingenuity was called for. Just before we left Cabo San Lucas we had purchased a large sack of limes, some brown sugar (the hard kind), and a few pints of stove alcohol. I had thought it might be needed to light our kerosene stove if the automatic lighter failed. Unplanned foresight resulted in a delightful concoction of white lightning and brightened the sunsets for the last third of the voyage.

I'm sure that our celebration at the equator will be strong in our memories for the rest of our lives. It is a tradition at sea that the first time you cross the equator you must be initiated into the Kingdom of Neptune. On any boat or ship, the initiation is done with grave, mock ceremony, and a lot of high jinks. In our case, Curt and I kept our pledge to shave off our beards. The two strangers who emerged from behind the bush went swimming after heaving Golden Fleece to and crawling into our safety harnesses. We took a cake of soap with us. We wanted to smell nice when we presented ourselves to Neptune's court.

Two white lightning cocktails later, we cooked a whole boned chicken over rice and ate it with my specialty, beer bread. A parting gift months ago had been a bottle of champagne. Ceremonially, we found two steel champagne glasses we had saved for this moment. We popped the cork, poured one whole glass into the sea for Neptune's enjoyment, asked him for fair winds and calm seas, then drank to His Eminence. If there is a god of the sea, I wonder what he thought of two naked men, half drunk, harnessed to their boat, saluting the Lord of Davy Jones' Locker?

For every navigator there is the thrill of his first landfall. One day my sights told me that we were right onto the latitude of Nuku Hiva, but I didn't know accurately how far east we were from our target. A squall line obscured the view, so I told Curt that we would heave-to. I didn't want to sail past the island. Since it was threatening to rain, we would wait until morning to find out if we were in sight when the weather cleared.

I got up at dawn, peered absent-mindedly out the hatch, then I saw a dark outline in the haze to the west. "Curt," I shouted, "come here and look, I think we have an island!" We were in a flat calm so I turned on the motor. I steered toward the shape on the horizon. Each hour the outline grew more distinct. Before long, we began to see green blotches and finally we were able to identify the land mass as Ua Huba, the island just east of Nuku Hiva. We had made it! We had done it on our own without Endurance's Sat Nav!

Coming in to Nuku Hiva's large bay was exciting when I turned on the VHF and heard a familiar voice come out of the speaker. It was Melba. "Golden Fleece, Golden Fleece, is that you Paul?"

We still had two or three miles to go but we knew we had reached our goal. The friendly sight of eight or ten yachts anchored in the bay was comforting.

An hour later, we dropped the anchor, unshipped the dinghy and rowed over to Endurance for some warm hugs and a warm beer—you get used to it!

Taiohae is a village of some several hundred

Polynesians and a few French administrators, and, of course, a number of Chinese shopkeepers. The business district is strung out along the waterfront and the homes are located in the two or three valleys that stretch up into this mountainous island. All stores are of the general variety stocking anything that the proprietor thinks will sell. There is a baker who makes that marvelous French bread fresh each day and you must shop for it in the morning or you lose out. Prices, except for bread, are two or three times those in Mexico and perhaps twice those in the U.S.

I had told Emily on the ham radio to send letters to general delivery (poste restante) in Taiohae. Eagerly, I went to the post office soon after checking in with the local gendarme, as is customary. There were several letters from Emily, and then the postmaster surprised me. "Golden Fleece?" he asked, then rummaged among letters and packages and found a big fat envelope. In it were letters from most of my high school classmates from my home town of Ainsworth, Nebraska. One of my classmates, "V.J." had organized a letter-writing project to greet me if and when I ever arrived in Taiohae. What a wonderful surprise that was!

As I walked back to the dinghy, I experienced a great feeling of pride that I, a senior citizen, a 65-year-old, had set out across a trackless sea, found a small island 2,500 miles later, and arrived healthy and fit! This and what followed was my dream, and I am writing to you today trying to share my pride and happiness. I was just a little saddened that my new bride had not shared in this triumph—but there will be many more adventures for us to share.

In three months and eight days she will join me in

in Papeete! I am very anxious for her to arrive.

    Love,
        Paul

City Park Papeete Saturday afternoon

3

Vavau,
Kingdom of Tonga
October 2, 1985

Dear Friends,

One of the happiest times in my life occurred when Emily came through the International Arrivals door at the Papeete Airport on Tahiti. She had a broad smile on her face and was the only woman coming through the door with a gasoline generator. During a phone call a week earlier, I had thoughtlessly suggested that she might purchase a generator and "just check it through with your luggage."

After suitable hugs and kisses we found a taxi and headed in to town. Dawn was just breaking as we drove in along the main road which paralleled the beach. I could feel the tension draining away as Emily contemplated her new life afloat. Palm trees were waving, the surf washed the beach, a light rain had dampened the pavements. Suddenly, as we were approaching the center of town, I told the taxi driver, "Stop here." He helped us unload our bags and carry them down to the beach where our dinghy, Lambie Pie, was drawn up. We loaded in the bags and rowed out to Golden Fleece which was only 30 or 40 yards out and tied to the shore, but held off the beach by a bow anchor. Thus, Emily approached the small vessel that was to be her future home.

The evening before, my neighbor had helped me decorate the boat. He donated a large banner he had used somewhere in the past that said, "I love you." I added the word "Emily" on a small piece of sail cloth. All the flags I possessed were flying from the mast and a strip of "used car lot" banner soared from the top of the mast down to the bow. I had hoped thereby to let her know that I was glad she was there. I think I succeeded.

Curt, as planned, had left Golden Fleece as soon as we had arrived in Papeete. He had been a good, willing, crewperson, but my new crew, although inexperienced, brought new meaning to my adventurous soul. Adventures, to be truly enjoyed, need to be shared, and I blessed again the fate that had brought Emily into my life.

The island of Tahiti is justifiably the Mecca for cruising sailors. It consists of two islands, Tahiti (the principal island), and Tahiti-iti ("iti" being the word for little), that are actually connected by a causeway. Papeete is like any other city of several thousand with traffic lights, rush- hour traffic, supermarkets, and hotels supplied by the huge jets that land and take off several times daily. It still contains much charm, however, because, from the sea, the island beckons with a shimmering green-blue luster, and, of course, palms flourish everywhere. There were a couple of whirly-cranes to mar the skyline and once a small plane flew over trailing a banner advertising something.

The open market was a delight. Almost every kind of vegetable was available, much to the delight of Emily, and the meat was plentiful and of excellent quality. The French baguettes, that slender hard-crusted bread, were delicious and always fresh, and Emily was ecstatic about the flaky croissants that only the French can make.

A second feature of Papeete that I found interesting was Le Trucks. These were privately owned taxi-buses that provided efficient, dependable transportation around the island. With them around, there was no need to own a car. Le Trucks went everywhere and the fares were reasonable.

The trucks were wooden, open canopies with seat benches along the sides. You boarded from the open rear and when you arrived at your destination, you walked forward and gave the driver-owner the required fare. The island was efficiently covered with good dependable transportation at no cost to the government, proving that private enterprise was working! And is working in many other "underdeveloped" countries, too.

Another of the joys of cruising is that you sometimes find yourself right in the middle of things. This is especially true for a sea-island culture such as you find in Tahiti. After Emily arrived, we anchored just off the beach of Papeete, the capital city of French Polynesia.

Despite its submission to TV, radio and modern schools, it still retains its ancient culture in song and dance. This is true partially because the tourists expect it and the competitive sea-oriented sports (canoeing, swimming and diving) that excite these young people who release their limitless energy thereby.

Emily and I were lucky to have picked the time around Bastille Day, July 14, so dear to the heart of Frenchmen, to set anchor. The date was an excuse for a big party by the Polynesians. Their party took the form of the Festival of the Arts of the Pacific. Invitations were sent to all of the Pacific island groups and delegations were sent from almost all of them except for the most poverty-stricken ones. For a week there was dancing, craft exhibitions, canoe races, and exhibits from the Cooks, Tonga, Fiji, Samoa, Vanuatu, and others.

We had a privileged view of the canoe races, the preparation, the practicing, and the finishes. Most of the teams launched their canoes from the beach just a few yards off our stern. There were single canoes manned by one, two, or four paddlers. The huge double canoes required eight paddlers. All the canoes were racing canoes, sleek, narrow, highly polished, and above all colorful. The double canoes paddled all the way to Moorea, about 15 miles, and returned.

In the Moorea race, when one crew had paddled for an hour, they would be relieved by a second crew, and then after resting, would return to work for another hour. The exchange process was fascinating. The motor vessel accompanying the canoe pulled ahead and the relief crew jumped into the water arranging themselves in a line. The double-hulled vessel was steered to straddle the line and a tired crew would roll over the outside. As the crew members struck the water, the relief crew swung aboard and picked up the paddles with hardly the loss of one stroke.

The first, second, and third canoes received a tremendous welcome for the five to six-hour ordeal. Our hearts went out to the last canoe that pulled in about dusk, to be met only by faithful wives and girlfriends who cheered the late-comers with affection.

The dancing exhibitions were held in an improvised stadium in the waterfront park on the central downtown quay. This quay was lined by yachts from all over the world moored stern-to on the waterside, and a busy thoroughfare on the city-side. In between, was mostly paved except for a few huge banyan trees. It was there that the amphitheater was erected and there were dancing exhibitions day and night. Each participating island's best dancers vied with the others for first-place honors. The dances varied from the shockingly erotic—swaying, lovely maidens and muscled, limber men—to marching groups. The costumes were colorful, the men and women beautiful and the music varied from wildly martial to haunting melodies.

We did not do much cruising around Tahiti or Tahiti-iti. We visited the Gauguin Museum by Le Truck. We purchased a case of Hinano beer, manufactured in Papeete and famous throughout the Pacific, and we did a lot of work on the boat. Emily, who was new to a sailor's life, did a lot of settling in. I am still amazed at what this little lady did. She quit a profession, packed all her former life in boxes and stored them. She turned her lovely house over to a realtor to rent and manage, boarded a plane lugging a generator that I had unfeelingly asked her to "just check through with your baggage," and packed two suitcases with everything she thought she would need in a small boat. With one life ending and a new one beginning, she flew 3,000 miles to a small island in the middle of a huge ocean to join a husband who left her the day after their wedding. Now, a few weeks later, she was happy, glad of the change in her direction and rapidly settling into a sailor's life.

I reflect now how lucky I am that, one, she chose to share my life, and, two, she had the amazing courage to do what she did. Frankly, finding such a woman is a rare thing. I have met many single men living on their boats and cruising who have been looking for a proper mate for years. Someone "up there" must like me.

We headed out for Moorea one early morning, on the first leg of our journey together. Moorea is west of Tahiti, downwind, of course, and we were hoping to experience more of the romantic South Seas as we dipped into the swells with the sun at our backs.

Our departure from Tahiti was Emily's first ocean passage. It was a blustery day and the seas were high but she stood it well and soon we ghosted in through the gap in the reef that protected the anchorage in Cooks Bay, Moorea. It is said to be the most beautiful bay in the world. I agree! We spent several days there enjoying the island and visiting friends whom I had met earlier in other anchorages. While we were there, we rented a motor scooter and climbed the hills on our put-put. As Emily rode behind me holding onto my waist, the machine flipped on a steep road gouging a deep wound in Emily's ankle. The local doctor treated the laceration and we thought little more of it, except that her ankle would be sore for a while.

From Moorea we went on to Huahine. This was Emily's first overnight passage. We stood watches and Emily took her turn like a trooper. A "watch" is a schedule of responsibility set up so that one person is awake and alert all night. We preferred two-on and two-off. Standing a watch consists of staying awake for two hours and checking the course and horizon every 15 minutes. If a ship was sighted, we would then need to watch it closely to make sure it was not on a collision course with our boat.

Huahine was not one of our favorite islands, mostly because of a dour postmaster and a Chinese shopkeeper who hustled me out of 500 francs. Most of the shopkeepers are purely honest and dependably fair—but there are a few who consider any tourist-type person fair game. To pay for my purchases I laid down a 1,000 franc note. I talked to Emily while he took care of another customer and there on the counter was my change—for a 500 franc note. I protested, he reached in the drawer and pulled out a 500 franc note and said it was the one I gave him. The conversation grew a little heated and he pretended not to understand English very well. He would not budge and so I finally stalked out. Needless to say, we spent little time in Huahine. Also, after lights out, a loud disco played until about midnight. Almost all the stores in French Polynesia are operated by Chinese who always spoke English, French, the local Polynesian dialect, and a polyglot form of Chinese. The stores carried a sparse selection of groceries and household items. The variety of goods depended on how long it had been since the last inter-island trader had been there. The traders were the inter-island schooners, small motor vessels of 500-1,000 tons.

From Huahine we had a good passage to Raiatea and Tahaa (pronounced TA-HA-A). These two islands were enclosed by a large coral reef.

A South Seas island reef grows slowly on the site of an ancient sea crater that has collapsed. Then, by the slow accretion of coral deposits, two cones form inside the reef creating the island, and a beautiful diverse cruising area.

As we approached Raiatea and headed in to the narrow hole in the reef, I had to leave the wheel to Emily who was terrified at being alone at the helm. I returned in plenty of time to steer us through the hole, but desertion in a moment of danger, no matter how urgent the reason, is not the way to treat your bride on her honeymoon. Once inside, we anchored near the town and the only quay on the two islands. We lingered a couple of days and then moved over to an anchorage at Tahaa.

This was much more pleasant but the holding was not good. After a restless night, we sailed to a small marina-harbor on Raiatea. Our neighbor there was a Frenchman who spoke good English. We had many pleasant chats with him (his wife was back in France) and Emily practiced her French on him. She spoke French wherever she could find a Frenchman or Frenchwoman to talk to. The cruising French are friendly, charming people who gladly and gently helped Emily with her language practice. Fondly, we remember a couple on a boat moored near us in Tahiti. They spoke slowly and clearly, so much so that even I, with just high school French, recognized a few words of their language.

From Raiatea it was an easy overnight sail to Bora Bora, the second most fabled of the South Pacific Islands.

Its reputation is justly deserved but somewhat dampened by the presence of a couple of huge hotel complexes. Thank goodness they were relatively unobtrusive. We spent all of our time there moored in front of the Hotel Oa Oa. This small complex consisted of only a few small cabins and catered almost exclusively to cruising yachtsmen like ourselves. They had some 20 moorings to tie to (all full when we got there), a dinghy dock, a bar, and a restaurant. The proprietors were former cruisers.

One of the fun events we experienced while we were there was the HOTEL OA OA CRUISING YACHT RACE. The rules were simple—there weren't any. We entered the race with the understanding that the skipper of each boat, with his crew waiting for him on board, would start the race with one hand planted on the bar at the hotel.

At a signal, the skippers would race for their dinghys, row out to the mooring, tie their dinghys to the mooring, scramble on board their boats, raise the sails, slip the mooring, and sail around a prescribed course. Their sails would be dropped when they returned to the mooring and the skippers would repeat their exertions in reverse. When they reached the bar, they were obliged to drink four beers. Placing the fourth empty bottle on the bar concluded participation and marked the time of the skipper.

I raced a Japanese fellow (whom I had first met in Mexico) to the bar for last place and we arrived almost simultaneously. I could not gulp down the icy cold beer. Neither could he. So we flipped a coin for our place. I won the toss and demanded to be counted as last. I wanted last place because the final loser was awarded a medal of paper and sea shells. This is the only medal I have ever won for sailboat racing!

While we were there at Bora Bora, Emily's ankle wound refused to heal and she developed a staph infection. She flew back to Papeete to enter a clinic which the Oa Oa proprietors recommended. The interesting fact is that the proprietors had not recommended the more expensive, "upper class" clinic for this type of problem, although we would have paid any price for a cure. The doctor at this "common folks" clinic took one look at her wound, and, professing no knowledge of English and ignoring her French, wrote out a prescription, handed it to her without a word and ushered her out. Within hours, the swelling had gone down, the pain had disappeared, and the next day she was back on Golden Fleece on Bora Bora. We have learned since that this infection is common in the islands and was frequently associated with coral scratches and cuts. So if you, my friends, plan a visit to the South Pacific, bring an old pair of canvas shoes for walking on the reefs.

Our entrance into Aitutaki Island in the Cook Island group was exciting. We appeared to be off the place where the chart indicated there was an entrance. We could see three sailboats anchored inside the reef but could not spot a way in. We got on the VHF radio and called to the boats. Sunchaser, whom we had met in Tahiti, answered and told us to head straight toward the reef on a course of 90 degrees.

With our hearts in our throats, we followed directions and soon encountered a small stake to which was attached a 5" by 5" black square. We saw the stake when we were only 50 meters from the reef. We followed a line of these stakes for about a quarter of a mile to deeper water inside the reef. There was never more than one foot of clearance under our keel and a couple of times we scraped the sand bottom.

We learned later that this channel had been dug by U. S. Armed Forces during World War II. Prior to that, nobody drawing more than one or two feet had ever been inside the reef. We anchored safely and soon discovered two of the three yachts were owned by friends from other anchorages.

We had several interesting experiences at Aitutaki. One of the funniest ones was "The Man in the Three-Piece Suit". Both Emily and I, from the vantage point of our freedom in the South Seas, had frequently expressed our disdain for those who stayed behind and toiled in their three-piece suits. Yuppies were the main object of our scorn for people whose lives were dedicated to acquiring "things."

We went to a hotel on Aitutaki—a restaurant and three cottages—and there, on a Friday, sampled the buffet dinner. Occupants from all three of the boats anchored were present. After our meal was completed, the tables cleared and moved to one side, a native orchestra came in. We danced for a while and were tickled by the maneuvers of an Aitutakin native with an Afro hairdo. He spoke no English but made Emily understand he wanted to dance with her. She obliged and whirled around the floor with the man in his three-piece suit—who wore no shoes!

Another touching event was when we went to the local church on Sunday. Emily put on a dress and her best flowered hat and we rowed in to the landing. We were ushered into the church in such a friendly manner that we felt that we were expected. We were taken to a vacant section of seats and greeted personally from the pulpit by the preacher in English. A skit was played in which two youths were portrayed, one a fine, devout young man and the other a dissolute wastrel. They both sought entry into heaven but the wastrel was denied entry because his "passaportee" was not in order. The deacons refused to pass the collection plate to us, we discovered later, because we were their "guests."

The Catholic priest in Aitutaki had maintained a log-notebook of all the visiting yachts that had sailed into the island. He was on his third volume. We added our names but did not actually get to meet the man because he was in Sydney in the hospital. The local storekeeper, who was also a ham radio operator, was keeping the log in the priest's absence. It was fascinating to browse through the log and occasionally run across the name of a yacht or captain that we knew personally or by reputation. The storekeeper loaded us up with the most beautiful eggplants we had seen before we left the island. His wife was a serious amateur horticulturist.

Another incident that was a bit sobering was when we and another couple decided to visit a wreck on the north side of the island. It was about two or three miles to the site. We started out in the Sunchaser's dinghy. The water inside the reef was only six to eight inches deep. So we were soon walking and pulling the dinghy, with lunch etc., behind us.

When we arrived at the wreck, it proved to be a beautiful teak yacht resting in about 12 inches of water. The hull, decks, and spars were sound except for a hole in the hull which two years of resting on the coral had ground through. It had been stripped of everything of value by the insurance company.

The story was that the owner and his wife were

having a bitter argument as they rounded the island and were not paying attention. The yacht, under automatic pilot, just sailed up on the reef. The waves were high and breaking and each wave moved the boat six or eight inches farther onto the reef. By the time the wind subsided, the yacht was a half mile from sufficient water to float her, but only one-fourth mile from the road.

We speculated on whether or not this beautiful hull could be salvaged, having heard that the insurance company was interested in offers. Our conclusion—impossible!

I remember suggesting to Emily that she and I save all arguments until we were at anchor. So far our honeymoon had been completely free of rancor. It was sad, too, to see here the end of someone else's dream. I sent up a silent prayer that our dream would not end in this manner.

We departed Aitutaki and headed for the Kingdom of Tonga, about five days away. The second day out, a storm blew up and we hove-to for about 36 hours. We just sat, going nowhere with the wind howling in the rigging and the boat pitching uncomfortably. We went below and held hands and prayed. This was the part of cruising that all sailors try to avoid but then brag about after it is over. We had just barely gotten underway again after the storm blew out when the backstay that holds the mast up collapsed.

Quick action on my part saved us from disaster as I rigged a temporary backstay. We tried to use the motor to control the boat and snagged a line around the prop. Next, the mainsail split and, finally, the stove quit working. This was not one of our good days!

Because of these minor disasters, we decided to put

in to Niue, a tiny island nation about 100 miles away and not far off our course. It was the closest landfall. Tonga, our destination when the storm came up, was about 500 miles away. There was no harbor or lagoon at Niue, but I discovered that, if the winds were not westerly, good shelter could be found in the lee of the island. We performed the repairs we required on the island and became acquainted with this fascinating tiny independent country.

The total population of Niue was only 2,700 and declining. There were no industries or resources although there were attempts to develop some. The soil was not rich. As a result, agriculture was poor except for copra which had a weak market. There was no harbor so there could be no fishing fleet. With no beaches, no tourists were attracted.

But the people were friendly and we even spent a leisurely half hour chatting with the prime minister. He was inspecting the work being done on the pier. The Australians had donated a couple of engineers and explosives for deepening the water alongside the pier. Holland had, just the previous year, donated a modest crane that was used to take loads off the lighters that brought stores in from the interisland freighters which anchored almost a mile offshore. For those who are looking for a place away from it all, Niue is the island. A nice small hotel offers comfortable accommodations.

While we were anchored there, a motorless sailboat, with its decks stacked with lumber sailed alongside us. They, we excitedly found out, were sailing to Aitutaki to salvage the yacht we had visited on the reef. These two young men and a third in New Zealand had purchased salvage rights from the insurance company and were going to attempt what Don (of Sunchaser) and I had agreed was impossible. They circled and came back and handed us some letters to mail and, having heard us on their receiver-only radio talking on the Amateur Radio Net, asked us to pass along a message to their partner in New Zealand who would be listening. This incident made us instant island celebrities. We went to the hotel for dinner and all of the staff and owner had observed the above incident and wanted to know what it was all about.

Before we left Niue, we talked with friends on the ham radio who were in Vavau, in the northern group of Tonganese islands. They strongly recommended that we come there first instead of going to the southern group as we had planned.

We had a good passage and, except for the fact that there was too little wind, arrived four days later.

We hoisted the "Q" flag in the harbor at Vavau and tied to the town quay. Soon the immigration and customs chaps came aboard and checked us into the Kingdom of Tonga with a minimum of fuss. By four in the afternoon, we were anchored off the Paradise Hotel, the most popular anchorage for yachts. We paid a dollar a day and got the run of the pool and showers and all the water we needed from the dock. The only irritating distraction were the "bumboats" piloted by vendors who came out to yachts to sell their fruit, shells, carvings, and baskets. They got to be annoying as they rapped on the side of the Golden Fleece often when we were settling down for a nap or dinner.

As we sat there on Golden Fleece, and as we had already met several boats who had been there for several weeks, we wondered how we could do justice to these "Friendly Islands," visit two more groups of the same, and make the two-week sail to New Zealand before Christmas. We were just too filled with wonderful life experiences and so overwhelmed with happiness that we regretted the limit that God had assigned to our life span. When you pass the three-score mark and your life is full, you want to hurry because there is so much left to see and do. The most satisfying factor in this whole equation is that I had found the perfect woman for these golden years. Apparently she had also found the perfect mate (I modestly submit) as she has not jumped ship yet.

    Keep well and happy!

    Love,
        Paul and Emily

MAFI

4

Opua, Bay of Islands
New Zealand
December 1, 1985

Dear Friends,

We arrived in this country on Thanksgiving Day; too late for turkey dinner we thought . Then we remembered that it was not our country and that its holidays had little to do with ours. Here is how we got to New Zealand.
Vavau, where we spent many lovely days, is part of a group known as the "Friendly Islands." These northern Tongan islands are not volcanic nor are they coral atolls.

They are composed of good, solid hard rocks and were formed by an up-welling of the earth's crust. There are none of the encircling reefs typical of the south seas, although there are many reefs visible in the island group and many coral white sand beaches.

The primary village is located on Vavau, the largest island, which also contains a nice hotel where you can anchor off the pier and use it as a dinghy dock. For this, and the use of the pool and showers, as well as unlimited fresh water for your boat, you pay $1.00 per day, Tongan dollars. The U. S. dollar, incidently, was slightly less in value!

One of the strongest memories we have of Tonga-Vavau is related to Vaha and Mafi, two natives we met. We were visited frequently on our first day on the island by Vaha, who rowed out to Golden Fleece in a leaky boat to sell us handicrafts. He invited us to visit his lagoon during the weekend and we arranged to meet him at the public pier.

The invitation was for Friday afternoon after he finished his work at the local shipyard. We met him at 3:30 p.m., and were greeted by him, his wife, Mafi, and six assorted teenagers. Mafi was a woman of jolly, round dimensions. When it was her turn to drop the few feet from the pier to the deck of Golden Fleece, I suddenly remembered something important to do on the foredeck. I admit I was a coward. I didn't want to be a party to her embarrassment as she tried to lower her bulk to the deck. When I looked back a moment later, she was planted firmly. To this day I wonder how she managed to descend. One theory is that the children made a sling with their arms.

Pear-shaped figures like Mafi's are considered beautiful in Tonga. A skinny wife indicates that her husband cannot feed his family properly. The conduct of the teenagers on the half-hour trip to Vaha's island was beautiful. They sang all the way. One of them would start a round of song and the others would pick it up. Like all Polynesians, their voices were harmonious and pleasant to hear.

Entering the pass into Vaha's lagoon was frightening. The guidebooks we owned warned of shoaling and a large rock in the entrance. Vaha, however, assured us that there would be no problem, so I gave him the helm and watched with trepidation as he aimed Golden Fleece on a course that seemed to kiss by the rock guarding the opening to the lagoon. Actually, my most anxious moment occurred after we got in and dropped the anchor. How were we going to get Mafi ashore? Our dinghy was a tiny one and if she sat on it, it would sink! My fears were stopped when I spotted an ample metal row boat putting out from the shore. Mafi went in on that, as did the rest of the crowd. From the boat we could see a small pier and a well-worn path leading up a slope, but no other sign of habitation. It was a lovely, unspoiled sight. Vaha had been right, we were enchanted by this place.

We agreed to meet the next day and spent part of the afternoon exploring. The next morning we waded in the shallow portions of the lagoon and examined the fish and plant life. We were startled when one of the fishes proved to be a poisonous sea snake. We stepped much more cautiously from then on.

At the appointed time of 11:00 a.m., we dinghyed to the dock and walked up the path of the slope.

There were no roads on the island, but we did see a few unhealthy looking horses who apparently served as local transport.

There was no orderly progression of houses. They seemed to have been put down casually with no plan or forethought and the path we were on wound through them. Each of the small cottages had one thing in common—a large concrete catchment tank to catch rain water. There was no fresh water spring on the island, we were later told, so the local noble had donated sacks of cement and sand to each family with instructions on how to construct the tank.

We found Mafi under a banyan tree weaving a large basket. The basket was for us; we had contracted for it in advance along with a few other items. As we sat in the pleasant shade with Mafi, Emily pulled out a sketchbook and started to make a sketch of one of Mafi's children. The child, apparently used to posing moved over close to Emily and stood perfectly still for 10 or 15 minutes.

When the sketch was finished, she examined it excitedly and then Emily noticed that another one of Mafi's children was posing in the same spot as the first. And so it went, one, two, three, four, five, before Emily was allowed to stop. Emily has made many friends with her sketchbook. She had captured the beauty, modesty, and courtesy of the Polynesian children.

Polynesian children are well behaved and amuse themselves. Mafi, the grand matriarch, would occasionally voice a mild admonishment and we noted that whatever the child was doing was stopped immediately. The eldest daughter was busy doing the laundry and told the younger children that she couldn't take time to be sketched. Emily sketched her busy at her task and then showed it to her. She was very pleased.

Soon we were invited in to share the family meal. The dwelling was a simple square frame building with a huge bed at one end and a table at the other. The parents slept on the bed and the children slept on mats here and there and frequently outside. All cooking was done in a shelter 10 meters away from the building and washing was done in another shelter nearby. There were no streets, just paths. In the afternoon, as we sat in the shade of the banyan tree, a dried-up old man came by on a withered old horse with a stalk of bananas balanced on his lap. A few words were exchanged between him and Mafi.

He got off the horse and came over and offered the stalk of bananas to us. To have refused would have been impolite, so we accepted enthusiastically. What we would have preferred was to cut off a couple of bunches, but he offered the whole stalk. The problem was that all the bananas would come ripe at the same time and there were only two of us to eat them. Most of our cruising friends had their own banana problems. We carried the stalk back to Golden Fleece when we returned for the night.

The next morning we met Mafi and Vaha and trudged off to church. The church was a small frame building with mats on the floor, a table at one end, and a small cabinet in the corner. A bed stood outside, obviously moved there to make more room inside. The preacher was a young man of quiet demeanor who conducted the service, not a word of which we understood, in an apologetic manner.

Vaha had explained that their church was composed of a group that had broken away from the main church on the island because of their dislike of the preacher. The preacher we were to meet was a lay preacher and would fill in until their nucleus could grow big enough to bring in a full-time preacher.

We sat cross-legged on the mats on the floor—not an easy task for my weary old bones. Soon after the service we returned to the boat, loaded on our former passengers and a few extra, and returned to the main island.

The Tongans are aggressive business people and harvest the tourist gold with vigor. On Vavau were two people who put on feasts. We attended both. Klepi, the more flamboyant of the two entrepreneurs, put on a feast at a local pavilion and featured the usual Polynesian foods: roast pork, octopus, crab, fish, poi, mangos, coconut, bananas and watermelon. We sat at a table and served ourselves from a sideboard. The dancers afterward were flamboyant and professional. We were particularly impressed by a fire dance in which a young man performed intricate maneuvers while whirling two or four flaming balls on the end of thongs.

The other entrepreneur was Aisea. His feast was the traditional one. We arrived early, having anchored just offshore, and dinghyed in. There was little sign of activity and no food cooking that we could see. Soon Aisea arrived with his slightly chunky wife and several musicians and girls in grass skirts whom we later learned were his daughters and a cousin. He and the musicians went over to a sandy place and started to dig and were soon uncovering leaves. Then rocks were uncovered and more leaves and there was our feast!

This cooking method has been followed for years and we felt privileged to help uncover the omu (the word for the ground oven). We carried packets of the food to the longhouse nearby and arranged them on a mat. Each guest then sat cross-legged and ate from a banana leaf with his fingers. After the feasting was over, the young girls came out to dance while the musicians played. They were cute and graceful and knew the movements well. The most charming dance was the solo performed by the younger of Aisea's daughters, about six or seven years old. She danced with great concentration and occasionally frowned at a mistake. Her mother was a bubbly person who could not contain herself when the music was playing and occasionally jumped up to dance a few steps to satisfy her overwhelming desire to express the call of the music. I understood her desire. I like to lead symphony orchestras—over the radio.

We were honored to be invited to Aisea's the next day to attend church and have lunch with them. The preacher on this occasion was a professional. He left little doubt in our minds about his message for the day—fire and brimstone and the wages of sin! He shouted, roared, and ranted. He made his voice small, dropping to an intimate whisper and stabbed his finger forcefully. Those sinners knew where they stood. We understood not one word, of course. The singing, as usual, was magnificent. At lunch we had the delicious leftovers from the feast the night before.

Just a word about the Tongan infra-structure. Tonga is, possibly, the only remaining absolute monarchy. The king rules by divine right. There is a parliament and a legal system and the king seldom interferes in day-to-day functions. He once overruled a life sentence handed down by the court and ordered the immediate execution of a particularly brutal murderer.

The laws are passed by a parliament of 18 people. The king appoints six people and the commoners elect six. The nobles form the other six. When you consider that the nobles exist by the grace of the king and could be reduced to poverty on a word from him, you can understand why things move so smoothly in Tonga, even if they are not always in the best interests of the country or its people.

The Tongans are the happiest of people in an ocean of happy people. They love and revere their king. I once asked a Tongan why he wore a grass mat wrapped around his waist. It didn't seem to serve any purpose. His reply was: "Out of respect for the king." Incidentally, routinely the men wear the lavalava—a wraparound garment that I found extremely comfortable and wore often around the boat. The women wear the traditional mumu, foisted on them years ago by missionaries, and carry umbrellas. They are the most dignified and majestic women I have seen anywhere. Emily is much impressed by them.

A typical scene is to see a boat being rowed across the water by a man or children while the matriarch sits erect under the shelter of her umbrella.

Each Tongan male receives about eight and one-half acres of fertile land and a building site in the village when he reaches the age of 18. The acreage is dispensed by the nobles who administer local laws and justice and collect taxes. Each noble rules a territory consisting of one or more islands. The Tongan nation was carved out when, about 300 years ago, one of the kings of the three Tongan island groups raised an army and conquered the other two groups. The kings who helped him were made nobles. I suppose they ate those they defeated.

We sailed south from Vavau to Nuku Alofa, the

southernmost of the three island groups of Tonga. We decided to skip the central group because of rumors of shallows and reefs. Also it was getting late in the season and we were approaching that time of year when hurricanes and tropical storms arrived. Our entry into the harbor of Nuku Alofa was a comedy of errors where we heaped speculation on bad judgement and stubbornness on top of poor decisions. We did not have a harbor chart, but on the island chart that we did possess the entrance to the harbor appeared to be clearly marked and easy to find. We sailed happily past a couple of active volcanos and watched an underwater eruption, finally arriving at what we thought to be the entrance.

We set course for the center of the island and started down a channel that was supposed to be 50 feet deep. Emily called some coral heads to my attention, passing near the boat. These devilishly fiendish protruberances are Davy Jones's way of keeping his locker full. They grow up from the bottom to within a few inches of the surface—but never in water 50 feet deep. Soon, stubbornness preventing us from reversing our course, we noticed that the 50-foot channel was only eight to ten feet deep and we were hopelessly lost in a sea of coral heads.

We sighted a couple of fishermen about a half-mile away and carefully threaded our way through the coral heads until we were close enough to speak to them. They spoke enough English so that we could ask directions, and with their assistance—they led the way for about a mile—we finally arrived in the 50-foot channel! From then on we had no difficulty and soon had the anchor down near the small marina in the main harbor.

The capital island and city of Tonga are called

Nuku Alofa and we spent two, very pleasant weeks there. We arranged for our sailing trip to New Zealand with the New Zealand embassy. New Zealand acts as a protectorate of Tonga, but wisely interferes not at all in the culture or government of the islands. The king loves to travel and spends most of his time flying around the world soliciting gifts from other countries.

One of the gifts from Australia was the loan of an economist for two years to advise the king. Carl was his name and he became our friend while we were on Nuku Alofa. Carl, who was nearing the end of his two years when we met, approached us on the quay and inquired after a boat that was anchored out. We agreed to look for it and to pass along a message he gave us. The next day he saw us again on the quay and we had a lengthy conversation followed by his invitation to come to his home and "just live ashore" for a couple of days.

The house and a servant for it were provided by the king and we lacked nothing in comfort and necessities. The highlight of our visit was a bridge party Carl was having in his home one of the nights we were there. We played with a diverse group whose members ranged from the British Ambassador to a member of the Rajneesh religious sect. We also played my first game of Trivial Pursuit, but it was the Australian version so Emily and I were excused from all questions pertaining to Australia. That may be the reason I won.

It was from Carl that we learned much about the king, and would have met him had he not been off somewhere in the world enjoying kingly privileges and perquisites. He loved chess, which Carl played well and often with him. The king told Carl that he preferred Carl's company because he could not associate with commoners and if he were to play chess with the nobles jealousy might result. It is lonely at the top.

Carl felt that his two years had really accomplished little with one exception. He had convinced the king to start a central bank system. Tongan funds had been held in Australian banks which paid a miserly amount of interest while they used the money to make more of it for the banks. A not uncommon practice.

By having its own central bank, all of the revenue would accrue to Tonga. Carl had made a study of the transportation system and recommended to the king that the Royal Tongan Airline, which the king wanted to start, should consist of several flying boats so that the islands of the three groups could be linked together. Despite the fact that there were no airfields on the islands, the king decided that he wanted gleaming jets similar to those in which he flitted around the world. The issue had not been resolved when we left. Carl was glad that he also was leaving because he did not wish to confront the king with the folly of his desire to buy big jets.

Soon the time to leave for New Zealand arrived. We had asked a young European lad, Ralf, to crew for us on the voyage because Emily and I did not want to stand watch continuously, as is required, on the high seas we would be crossing during the passage. With three of us taking turns at watch everyone was allowed two four-hour off-watch periods in every 12.

Our voyage to New Zealand was normal. There was one storm that we sat out for two days hove-to. Our Sat-Nav was working perfectly, after having produced questionable results since its installation in the Marquesas.

When that happened, we called the factory in England and were informed how to correct the problem. We did, however, drift a little too far to the east on the 14-day trip to New Zealand and were afraid that we would have to buck the wind to make enough westing to reach our landfall—the Bay of Islands. Fortunately, the wind died as we approached the North Island and we had to motor for 36 hours to make the landfall.

Making a landfall is one of the greatest thrills a sailor can enjoy. We thought that we should be able to see Cape Bret about two in the morning. Emily was on watch at 0130 in the morning and woke me to report a flashing light on the horizon. We timed it with a stop watch and, yes, it was the Cape Bret light! Since the range of the light was 25 miles, I went back to bed secure in the knowledge that we wouldn't be near the land for another four or five hours.

We learned that our crewman, Ralf, preferred to be called Alofi, a Tongan name he had adopted while he was living on the island of Vavau with the native Tongans. He was a former travel agent in Germany and at 21, after serving his apprenticeship in the travel business, decided to see the world and learn more about the people of the South Pacific. The reason he wanted to go to New Zealand was to live with the Maoris on that island, get to know them better, and learn to speak their language. We made a new friend in Ralf and often wonder about him. He was tough, in the physical sense. Although mildly seasick during the entire two-week voyage to New Zealand he insisted on standing his watches and wouldn't allow me to go out on the foredeck—insisting that it was his job.

We entered the Bay of Islands, which is just that, a

huge bay dotted with many islands which promised many days of fine cruising and sailing. It was December, down under, and the weather was hot. When Santa arrived in a few weeks he would be overdressed among the sunbathers.

We docked at Opua, a small settlement at the southern end of the bay, and cleared customs. New Zealand has strict laws on food imports. The customs officer brought a huge plastic bag with him into which we were required to put all of our fresh vegetables and fruit. We could have cooked them and then he would have let us keep them. He offered to return in a half hour if this was our desire. We were anxious to get the procedure completed and could see no great financial advantage to cooking four potatoes and three apples. We were required, also, with no options, to put all canned meat in his sack unless it had been canned in New Zealand. The customs agent was a fine young man, pleasant and courteous, and just reinforced our strongly held feeling that we were going to have a wonderful time in this country.

Now as we contemplate Christmas in this antipodal setting, our thoughts go out to you, whom we love. We hope that you celebrate with your family and loved ones and that your Christmas is a very merry one.

    Love,
        Paul and Emily

5

Wellington,
New Zealand
March 12, 1986

Dear Friends,

    As I write this we are sitting in a travel trailer (called a "caravan" in New Zealand) awaiting the settlement of a strike so that we can proceed on a long-planned tour of the South Island of New Zealand. As most of you know, New Zealand consists of two islands appropriately called the North Island and the South Island. They are separated by the Cook Straits, venerating the man much admired all through the North and South Pacific,

Captain Cook. You may recall that the Hawaiians liked him so well that they ate him.

The strike I speak of prevented us from crossing the straits to the South Island. In our tour of the North Island, we had reserved a trailer, excuse me, caravan, in a small town just north of Wellington called Papatoetoe (pronounced papa-toy-toy). We had hoped to cross the straits before nightfall and camp on the South Island. The stewards of the ferries decided that they were not getting paid enough, so they refused to report for work. They operated the concessions on the ferries and were not essential to the sailing of the ferries. However, the captain and crew decided to support them so we settled down in the caravan park until things were restored to normal.

We were thoroughly enchanted by New Zealand and its people. The New Zealanders refer to themselves as Kiwis, after the flightless bird that is almost extinct but is still found in pockets on the islands. Some, including the Kiwis themselves, say that New Zealanders are more British than the British. We saw no evidence to dispute this view. When we were in Wellington previously, we just missed seeing Queen Elizabeth. She had opened Parliament, a practice still persisting from the colonial days, although usually done by the local commonwealth representative. Schools were dismissed and the Queen's and her consort's ribbon cutting and other activities were daily headlined in the press.

Rugby, cricket, tennis, bowls, horse racing including trotting, and soccer are the principal sports. There are tea rooms everywhere. I developed a profound respect for a ceremony called Devonshire Tea. It took sixteen dishes to perform it and included scones, jam, and clotted cream. The problem was that it all went to waist.

Since I wrote to you last we have enjoyed the cruising community, toured the North Island and generally learned to appreciate this wonderful country. Let me start by describing our activities in the cruising community.

The Bay of Islands is a large body of water dotted with islands near the north end of the North Island. We anchored, as did most of the group that crossed the South Pacific, near a small town called Opua. There were perhaps 30 or 40 cruisers anchored or tied to buoys. The buoys were either owned by individuals or rented by the harbormaster to cruisers for $1.00 (NZ) per day. One of the buoys was owned by a famous cruising couple, Eric and Susan Hiscock. They came into the harbor about a month after we got there, but then went on to Auckland where Eric was hospitalized.

The cruisers soon developed into a friendly, close-knit community. Each morning at 0800 we participated in an inter-ship network on the VHF radios. We all took turns running the net as, of course, someone had to be in control. The controller called the roll and gave each boat an opportunity to speak. We exchanged messages, recipes, gossip, news, and announcements.

On one occasion, after we were notified by mail that we had been elected Commodores of the prestigious Seven Seas Cruising Association, we announced a party at 1700 (5:00 p.m.) for the first hoisting of our Commodore's burgee (flag). Several other SSCA Commodores in the fleet came over and enjoyed the moment. Our one bottle of champagne and our two stainless steel wine glasses stretched over the occasion nicely.

We, the cruisers, were welcomed into the local

community by being made temporary members of the local yacht club. They gave parties and we were all invited as members. We used their clubhouse, a former union hall when Opua had been more active than now. We had our meetings there, we had some parties of our own and took advantage of the shower facilities. The hall had showers but were not marked "MEN" and "WOMEN" because the former occupants of the building were all men. So— shower time was designated between 1600-1800 hours (4-6 p.m.). We paid 50 cents for the hot water. This meant that each day we, the cruisers, had to call for volunteers to monitor the showers. This meant the responsibility for unlocking the club, collecting the 50 cents per person, and making sure that men didn't burst in upon women showering, and vice versa. Married couples were allowed to shower together, of course. A part of the daily radio net agenda was to obtain the shower monitor for the day.

    An activity that I became involved in was an effort to re-galvanize our anchor chains. In salt water the galvanizing will last only three or four years before rusting, and then, since the steel is okay, it can be re-coated with a non-rusting metal made of a lead alloy. One of the members discovered that if we galvanized 1,000 kilos (about one ton) of chain at one time that we could save as much as 34 cents per kilo. He mentioned this on the morning net. Someone else suggested that we organize a galvanizing effort since many others needed to have their chains galvanized, also.

    The outgrowth of this was that I was given the title of Admiral in Charge of Galvanizing. On the appointed day, all the yachts involved brought their chains to the pier in their dinghys. Some dinghys were nearly awash, the chains were so heavy. I gave each chain an identification number so that it could be returned to its rightful owner as all chains look pretty much alike. A truck from the plant arrived and we loaded on, not one, but two thousand kilos of chain. It all turned out okay and only one skipper was disappointed. I had an anxious moment when another skipper picked up his chain and was sure that it was 50 feet shorter than when he had sent it. Then he remembered that he had only bought 250 feet originally, but had planned to buy 300. Can you imagine the effort involved in trying to find the "other" chain on 18 different yachts?

One of our young crew members was getting his schooling by correspondence and the tests for each year had to be administered by any qualified school professional. The local Opua grammar school agreed to take the responsibility and a date was set for the exam. The entire fleet was sweating it out for him (he was nine) and on the morning of the exam we all wished him good luck and other assurances on the VHF net. P.S. He made it! And we knew he would. Incidentally, we have met a lot of children cruising with their parents. They are all intelligent, way ahead of their contemporaries in the States and mature far beyond their years. The cruising life is good for kids.

Another incident which I frequently recall with a smile is the "stroking kiwi" incident. A group of us went to a nearby national forest to participate in a "kiwi walk." The forest ranger guaranteed that we would see a kiwi during the walk. We met at 10:00 p.m. because the kiwi is a nocturnal bird and is seldom seen during the day. We carried flashlights, which we used sparingly, and followed the ranger into the forest hardly daring to breath in excited anticipation of seeing this shy bird whom many Kiwis (of the human species) have never seen in the wild. The kiwis were quite prolific at one time, and they had no natural enemies until the Maoris arrived. The giant moa, another flightless bird of ostrich proportions, became extinct. Having no fear of man it was easily hunted for food. The decimation of the smaller kiwi, which is about the size of a small chicken, was partially due to its food availability, but its major predation is a result of the destruction of habitat and the family pets introduced by the Europeans. A valiant effort is being made by all New Zealanders to preserve and enlarge the small population of kiwis that remains. A small group lived on the wooded hillside near our boat and could be heard whistling during the night.

But on with the story. The ranger played a recording of kiwi calls on a portable tape recorder, but the midnight deadline approached and we had neither seen nor heard a kiwi. We trekked disconsolately back toward the van that had brought us to this section of the forest when suddenly the ranger said "Stay here!". He crashed into the forest and was heard moving about in varying directions. Finally a shout, "I got him!" Our respect for that young man doubled as he stepped out onto the path carrying a feathery bundle.

He held him, or her as the case may have been, down on the ground and invited us to stroke him and especially to feel the point where the vestigial wings were located. The next morning on the VHF net I felt compelled to report on the great pleasure we had had the previous night and my delight at having actually stroked a kiwi. Out of the air, came an unidentified voice saying, "I stroked an 18-year-old Kiwi fast night." The owner of that voice had an unmistakable British accent, but I could never get him to admit to having said that. His wife, however, winked at me while he was vehemently denying any complicity.

It seemed to be a rather common practice among the cruisers at the Bay of Islands to purchase a car when they arrived and sell it later when they left to return to the islands of the Western Pacific. Usually it was sold for about the same as they paid for it and, in the interim six months or so, enabled them to tour the country and to make frequent shopping trips to nearby Paihia, Kawakawa, and Whangarei. We bought a small Ford of sufficient power to pull a small trailer with which we planned to tour the South Island. The most popular car was a tiny Ford with a small engine that was about two steps up from a motor scooter, but which had surprising accommodations. We chose a larger car for the reasons mentioned. We would, of course, announce on the morning net when we planned to go to Paihia, Kawakawa or Whangarei and offer rides for two.

We purchased our car one Friday afternoon in Kawakawa, drove it home, parked it, and, I think, locked it, and dinghyed out to our boat. The next day about midmorning, the man who had sold us our car arrived in a dinghy and informed us that our car was in the ditch about 40 kilometers south. The police had found it there and, since the dealer was still the registered owner, had called him. Apparently some scalawags, the term used by the officer, had borrowed it and gone for a joyride. Not many people can claim that their new car was stolen the first night of its purchase.

As planned, we toured the North Island with our friends Don and Geri on Sunchaser. We returned with some strong impressions of this delightful country. The North Island is a beautiful and friendly country. It is green and generally hilly, but liberally sprinkled with flat, fertile valleys. The interior contains a few large lakes and one volcanic peak on the west coast that has a skiing facility on it. There is a volcanic area midway on the island containing some rather spectacular geysers and other volcanic phenomena. Auckland, the largest city, has a fine harbor which opens on the east, or Pacific coast, while some of the suburbs face the Tasman Sea on the west coast—so narrow is the island at this point.

Wellington, the capital city, fronts on the Cook Straits, has a good harbor, and is a colorful city. It is dominated by the "Beehive," the building that houses the national government. Quite frankly, it looks like a beehive and is the product of the efforts of a recent head of state who was an architect. The entire country is divided into two camps; those who think that it is hideous and those who think it is marvelous.

The people are friendly, outgoing, and helpful. Emily was looking for the "loo" (New Zealandese for restroom. British too.) in a tiny mountain town. She paused before a forbidding and confusing structure. A passing lady in a car shouted, "It's around in back, dearie." This is a typical New Zealand gesture. Everywhere people go out of their way to be helpful.

Another time we were shopping in Kawakawa and entered a shop. The proprietor did not have what we wanted but said, "Come with me." She left her own shop, walked several doors down the street, entered another shop and told the proprietor what it was that we wanted. Later, as we were backing out of a difficult spot on the main street, a smiling man stepped out and held up traffic until we were clear.

New Zealand is a neat country. Houses are neat, painted, and often trimmed with colorful, well-kept flower beds. There are hedgerows between fields and tall dramatic poplars line the fence lines between neat, well-tilled fields. Here and there we saw large plantings of exotic trees (our own Pacific Northwest Douglas fir being favored for these artificial forests). The Kiwis are, wherever possible, replacing the forests that were logged so rapaciously long years ago.

The islands were once covered with the kauri tree, a very fine ship-building wood which was much sought after. Indiscriminate cutting nearly denuded the islands of this fine tree and the clearing for sheep ranching completed the rape. The reforestation is a fine attempt, where possible, to restore as much land as possible to the climatic beneficiality of forests.

There are sheep everywhere. They dot the hillsides like tufts of cotton. It is said that there are 3,000,000 people and 30,000,000 sheep. We saw no reason to deny this.

There is a delightfully mature beef-dairy industry here in spite of the dominance of the sheep. New Zealand cheddars will rank with the best in the U.S. and one of the best steaks I have _ever_ eaten was at the Opua yacht club. Strangely enough, in spite of all the sheep, you can find plenty of mutton and leg of lamb but lamb chops are hard to find and you must visit several shops before you find some. In the hotels and motels you are nearly always presented with a complimentary bottle of milk.

The cities are a wonderful mixture of modern buildings and ancient landmark edifices. They, the Kiwis, are quite history and culture conscious. The Maoris first came to the islands about 800 AD, probably from the Marquesas. By 1896 their population had declined from probably 100,000 to only 42,000 thanks to the diseases the Europeans brought with them. Now some 270,000 Maoris are politically active, have recovered some of their land, and their culture is preserved in museums everywhere.

A couple of kilometers north of Paihia at a place called Waitangi is the official headquarters and home of the Maori nation. Their longhouse is a thing of beauty and is adorned with elaborate carving. The Maoris not only carved the beautiful warm kauri wood, but were excellent jade carvers also. The wood carvings invariably contain the head of a typical Maori warrior with his tongue sticking out. This was supposed to strike fear into the hearts of their enemies.

One of our most dramatic experiences was when the double canoe sailed in from Hawaii. This voyage was accomplished totally in the manner of the ancient Polynesian navigators, an art that is reviving just in time. The last of the ancient navigators were dying off, replaced by satellite navigators, sextants, and other sophisticated modern devices.

The Maori chief, dressed in his bird feather cape and standing tall and dignified, went out in the official canoe of the Maoris. This is a magnificent work of art which holds 52 people at least. It is kept under a covered shed on the beach at Waitangi and taken out into the bay on ceremonial occasions. Imagine the scene that we witnessed as we sat on our boat waiting for the meeting. Twenty-five brawny, dark Maori men on each side with white paddles flashing in the sun. The 51st person was the coxswain whose chants carried out over the water, and the men responded with the chant. The paddles flashed, or were reversed, or were put at ease in the air in perfect unison. The chief stood proudly in the bow as the canoe slowly and delicately approached the twin canoe from Hawaii. With stateliness befitting a true monarch, the chief stepped aboard the canoe to welcome these voyagers from afar. Out stepped the captain of the Hawaiian craft dressed in shorts, dirty sneakers, and a T-shirt. He probably forgot to pack his bird cape.

The political-economic structure in New Zealand is about 50 years behind ours in the U.S. The labor unions have yet to learn that they cannot ride roughshod over the rights of the general public. A benevolent welfare state is just waking up to the fact that maintaining the present course will bankrupt the nation, and in the meantime the politicians bicker over nonessentials while doing little about the big problems. The current head of state is making some effort to privatize some state-owned industries while he attempts to create a nuclear-free South Pacific by denying U.S. military vessels access to New Zealand's harbors.

The entire nation is oriented toward the sea and sailing. New Zealand firms sponsored two entries in the Whitbread Around the World Race. No U.S. firms could be persuaded to give other than token sponsorship to our one entry. We just missed the start of the third leg of the race out of Auckland. We were told that the vast harbor was covered, literally, with yachts who had come to see the competitors off. One of the worlds great yacht designers is a Kiwi. Almost every businessman we met wanted to talk about sailing and his boat—including the man from whom we purchased our car.

During the tour that we made of the North Island, we stopped at a place called the Agridome. It promised a lecture on sheep, a shearing demonstration, and a demonstration of sheep dogs in action. The director was a man called Ivan who claimed to be a six-time national shearing champion. He was also an excellent showman. Days later we had a chance to attend a national championship shearing competition in a town not far away, but didn't think we could spare the time required. After all, we had watched a champion perform. After Ivan had produced the fleece from the sheep, accompanied throughout with a charmingly clever dialogue, he asked two ladies to come up and hold it up for the audience to see. The two ladies he selected were Emily and Geri. They are now enshrined in film in many cameras, including ours.

The other part of the show that was very instructive was his discussion of the various breeds of sheep. Each breed, and there were 19 displayed, was called out through a door and mounted a dais assigned to him. They then stood patiently until the show was over. I was not aware that there were so many breeds, each bred for a purpose.

Then we all trooped outside to watch a sheep dog demonstration. These intelligent animals were absolutely amazing. I had seen them before in the highlands of Oregon, but because of brush obscuring their movements, had little idea of how important they were to the shepherd.

The town of Hamilton at about 100,000 population was one of the most attractive cities I have ever seen. Most of the towns in New Zealand have been built in the European style with a large square in the center. Hamilton's town center is beautifully and tastefully landscaped with statues, banks of brilliant flowers, and a carillon tower. The square is surrounded by beautifully maintained older buildings, most in a light, but tasteful, rococo gothic. Spotted here and there were modern buildings of glass and slate, but all well designed and tastefully landscaped. Adding color to the large paved portion of the square were flower carts with gay awnings. We loved Hamilton.

We are learning to speak New Zealandese. The local postmistress, Margaret, was a friend of all of us yachties and knew us all by sight. Sometimes we didn't understand her or the keeper of the small store—Bev. Bev's name was "Biv" spoken quickly and curtly. "Yis," spoken in the same manner translates as yes. "Bird" is a girl, especially a pretty one. "Good on ya" translates as nice going, and "solid gold" means that what you are doing meets with approval. All this in a clipped speech spoken through tight lips. Strangely enough, a New Zealander told me that he thought it was remarkable that the only place in the world where English is spoken without an accent was right there in New Zealand. Odd, I thought it was in central Nebraska.

Some of the delights of cruising in the Bay of Islands are worth mentioning. There are many islands, as you might suspect, most with lovely beaches and many of these are rich in pipis. The pipi is a small mollusk resembling a clam that lives in the shallows in the coarse sand. You gather them by dipping your fingers in the sand and then washing it away. The pipis remain. You steam them for a few minutes, dip in sauce, and enjoy one of the finest of hors d'oeuvres. They are especially delicious while splicing the mainbrace after the sun is past the yardarm (a salty way of saying "cocktails").

We went on a local cruise with the yacht Sunchaser

up the Kerikeri River. Let me interrupt to tell about cruising friends, especially Don and Geri. After you have run into another yacht several times during your drift across the ocean, you develop a fondness for the company of some yachts over all of the others—sort of like real life, eh? Don and Geri were those kind of people for us. Geri enjoyed poking through tide pools, one of Emily's favorite pastimes. Don knew the same tired jokes and ribald camp (Boy Scout) and Navy songs that I did. We also had a running feud going with the cribbage board. The two women also enjoyed exploring the shorelines in Lambie Pie, our dinghy. So it was not surprising that we planned a cruise up the Kerikeri together.

Two years ago several yachts were lost on the Kerikeri by a flash flood that roared down the river laying waste both right and left. One of the buildings that survived the flood was the Old Stone Store located several miles up the river. With the exception of some T-shirts and some post cards it was pretty much the same as when it was built in 1833. Now a national landmark it is maintained, probably at a loss, by the state. Not many people buy their crackers from a barrel or their vinegar from a keg, etc. We motored up the river and anchored in a small pool near the store.

While there, we had several experiences, such as walking into the town of Kerikeri. On the way back we purchased kiwi fruit and oranges from an unattended roadside stand. The prices were posted and there was a can into which you dropped your money and made change. The kiwi fruit were, I think, about 15 cents (NZ) and the oranges about five cents. We stopped at the orchard of a yachting friend and picked up all the windfall oranges we could carry.

This friend we had seen at the island of Niue when we were there. They had sailed by and given us a letter to post. They also asked us to report their location on the ham radio. They were on their way to Aitutaki in the Cook Islands to salvage a yacht there. They had succeeded and had repaired it well enough to bring it back to New Zealand, but were looking for a motor and other necessaries in order to make the voyage. Imagine our surprise when he rowed up to Golden Fleece and said, "Remember me?"

Our second experience also involved this young man. After we had been there for a couple of days it started to rain—and it rained—and rained. In the middle of one of the heaviest downpours, the young man rowed out and suggested that the storm was similar to the one that had caused the disaster and we would probably be wise to put out and anchor in the bay. It was interesting to see the five yachts that were in that pool wending their way down that river in a tempestuous storm. We went out into the bay and, with Sunchaser, elected to stop at the small bay off the large bay to anchor for the night. The others went back to Opua. With the rain hammering down on the deck overhead, and after a bowl of hot soup, we settled down for the night, snug in our bunks.

I mentioned the volcanic area in central North Island. During our tour we explored this area which, in many ways, was reminiscent of our Yellowstone Park in Wyoming. There were geysers, bubbling mud, steam, and smelly pools. One geyser with a perfect small cone, apparently erupted on command, because the eruption time of 10:00 a.m. was painted on the permanent sign out in front. Mother Nature must have been subordinate to Father Nature in New Zealand, we thought. This geyser was called the "Lady Elizabeth" geyser.

The story was, according to the ranger who appeared promptly at 10:00 a.m., that a British diplomat's wife, who was camping nearby, decided to do her laundry in the convenient hot water that lay quietly inside the cone. She tossed in her clothes and then some soap. About 60 seconds later the geyser erupted, sent clothes flying every which way. The ranger then dumped in a cup of detergent and a few white cloths into the cone. Almost exactly 60 seconds later we were treated to a spectacular spout of water, steam, and strips of white cloth! The relaxation of the surface tension of the water by the detergent is the cause of the eruption.

Another fun phenomenon of the area was the "Hot Beach." There was, apparently, a volcanic spring under the sands of the beach which caused an upwelling of fresh, hot water. There were spots on the beach where it was painful to walk. In the more moderate areas the bathers could scoop out depressions that would fill quickly with hot water. One could enjoy all the comforts of a hot tub, without the jets, of course.

If my enthusiasm for this country has motivated you to investigate living here, here are a few facts of reality. You cannot just immigrate to New Zealand. If you are not retired with a fixed income, you must have a skill that is needed in the country. Most professionals, except lawyers, are welcomed as are most of the skilled trades. The country was facing a high (12 percent) unemployment rate when we were there, and did not need more unskilled or semi-skilled citizens. Prices were moderate but taxes were high, as is to be expected in the socialized countries. Would we live there? Joyfully, if we did not have so many friends such as you in the U.S.

Keep well and happy.

Love,
      Paul and Emily

Young spectator – Opua days celebration

6

Las Vegas,
Nevada
June 29, 1986

Dear Friends,

    Yes, this is being written in Las Vegas, the Tinsel Town of America. Don't jump to the possible conclusion that we came here to fatten our cruising kitty. My sister, Joanna, better known as Jo, and her husband, Merril, frequently called Bob, live here and we are visiting them. Actually, we find this type of entertainment and hype and glitter almost alien after spending the last couple of years in a quite, slow, nearly primitive environment, such as the

South Pacific. We do enjoy the long passages between islands that last several days or weeks. There is a serenity and kinship with nature out there that is good for the mind. Far from the "madding crowd" the wild-life is abundant, strangely enough, the air is clean and from horizon to horizon is the entire world. The weather is, admittedly, sometimes frightening, but no more dangerous to a stout ship than the freeway is to others.

Las Vegas, on the other hand, represents the opposite end of the spectrum. There, all the sins are available, for a price of course, and they all scream for your attention. I guess we just dance to a different drummer.

In our tour of the North Island we stopped in a small suburb of Auckland called Papatoetoe and reserved a small trailer that was not too heavy to be towed by our little Ford. On our way to South Island we stopped and hooked up our trailer, planning to cross the Cook Straits before stopping for the night. Unfortunately, this was not possible because of a strike of the stewards on the ferries. We found a small trailer court nearly full with people in the same fix and settled in for the night.

The next day no progress was reported in the talks, but about 3:00 p.m. we were informed that the ferries would start running in about an hour. We quickly unhooked our umbilicals and got in line. The first ferry filled before we reached the front of the line, but we made it onto the second. The problem was that we were towing a trailer and this put us in a separate category for which there were only a limited number of spaces. Happily, we crossed the straits, landed, and then discovered the small settlement at the ferry dock had two trailer rental businesses well stocked with small trailers. Apparently knowledgeable people do not rent on the North Island to tour the South Island.

We had planned to make a trek (hike) of the Milford Sound area but the ferry strike delayed us, so we had to cancel the hiking reservation we had made. Since the number of people allowed on the trail was limited, the next opening was six weeks away! We decided instead to visit a cruising friend whom we had met in the Pacific who was now living in Christchurch.

Warren was a radiologist and was spending two years working and teaching at a hospital in Christchurch. He had elected to get there by sailing his boat, "Bilbo Baggins," and taking a year to do it.

Warren told us about an amusing incident that happened to him while he was in the Cook Straits. He lost a shroud (the steel cables that hold the mast upright) and radioed for help. By the time a rescue boat arrived he had jury-rigged the mast in such a way that he felt confident he could make the trip on to Christchurch without help. He informed the rescue boat by radio that he didn't need its help, but the captain insisted that he allow a line to be attached to his boat and be towed in. There were several television cameras at the Auckland pier when the rescue boat pulled in with Bilbo Baggins in the rear. The captain explained to Warren apologetically that the rescue boat had been purchased, at great expense, six months earlier, but so far, until Warren, had rescued no one. People were beginning to grumble that the boat was wasted money. Would Warren pretend he had been helpless in order to mollify public opinion? Warren agreed.

As we hurried south toward Christchurch, we were treated to marvelous vistas of rocky coast with scenes of seals sunning themselves. Two other impressions stayed with us: the steepness of the mountain terrain and the trains scurrying along the coast.

The mountains were nothing more than large hills by western U. S. standards, but they were steep and numerous, seldom broken by any kind of plain, and suitable only for grass growing and sheep grazing.

The trains that darted in and out of the many tunnels along the coast were four-wheeled, resembling the "forty and eights" of World War I. The operators were young and friendly and waved to us as they passed.

Christchurch was a quaint mixture of old and new with careful attention to the preservation of natural assets and historic buildings. It is located on a beautiful bay on the east coast about one-third of the way down the island. A clear, meandering stream, the Avon, flows through the middle of the city and is beautifully landscaped with a walk, weeping willows, well-mowed grass, and ducks. A picturesque square is lined with a mixture of department stores, a huge old cathedral, flower carts, and historic buildings that were constructed a century ago.

Warren was house-sitting for a colleague and invited us out to have dinner with him. The house had a grand view and was decorated with magnificent paintings. Emily and I feasted on scenery, a marvelous salad, contemporary artists, and friendship for a memorable evening. The heavy rain that we encountered on our way back to the trailer did not dampen our spirits.

The next morning we headed to a rendezvous at a Halley's Comet viewing site where we had a reservation. It was still raining and the local radio warned of flooding in the lowlands. As we moved across the alluvial plains of

Canterbury (yes—Canterbury—the Kiwis have a penchant for British names), we drove carefully through a few "water on the road" places. Soon, however, we were forced to drive through a long puddle about one-quarter mile wide with only fence posts in sight to guide us. Ahead we saw a village on high ground. We steered for it and soon pulled in to a small trailer court with a sigh of relief. At least we would have company if we were going to be swept out to sea.

The next morning we found that our village had been isolated and surrounded by water. This little town of Geraldine was an island and there were no roads out. We accepted the inevitable and settled down to await the recession of the waters. Noah couldn't have picked a better place. The locals were solicitous about our welfare. Local farmers with cows to milk were distributing milk in the town square (bring your own container).

We spent a lot of time listening to radio Caroline (the district in which the little town of Geraldine was located). It was the sole link with the outside world. The local announcers devoted much of their time to special bulletins and messages to relatives.

We heard the heart-warming story of the rancher who was preparing to abandon his house to the rising water and remembered his beloved sheep dogs. He went out to where they were tethered and saw them in water over their heads swimming energetically against the current. They knew the master would come and rescue them!

Soon a bridge was restored and we were able to exit Geraldine to the north. Not far away was the resort area of Hanmer where we decided to go while things dried out. While we were there, we took a sixhour hike through natural forest and planted forest. It was there that we gained respect for the Kiwis' sensitivity to the environment and their herculean efforts to restore and preserve. We could look across a wide valley at several square kilometers of planted forest.

It was near there one night that I was feeling restless and went outside for some fresh air. There in the sky, head, tail and all, hanging just over the tip of a pine tree, was Halley's Comet. We had tried to sight it before, but haze, clouds, and perhaps some confusion over the directions in the news- papers, prevented our being sure that we saw it. Although we saw it many more times in the days ahead, those sightings were not as satisfying as the one that night when I ran in and woke Emily with the news that the comet was blazing in the sky.

We did go on to the comet viewing area in the highlands, after the roads had been repaired. We met experts who assembled us in an old shearing shed on a ranch and greatly enhanced our knowledge of astronomical phenomena. When we went outside to prepare to view the comet through high-power telescopes and binoculars, a small cloud blocked our immediate view so we walked around waiting for it to go away. Finally, when we were chilled to the bone and just at dawn, the cloud disappeared, but it was too late. The dawn light destroyed the contrast necessary to see the comet, and we all left—much disappointed.

Our next objective, higher into the mountains, was Mount Cook, New Zealand's tallest peak. We passed many grand vistas, saw thousands of sheep and, as I mentioned in my last letter, came to admire the sheep dogs performing their guardian tasks. Up high on Mount Cook there is a statue of a sheep dog that venerates the importance of the breed to the economy of New Zealand. When we arrived at the lodge near Mount Cook we took a plane ride and landed on Abel Tasman Glacier—the longest glacier in the world. For me, standing in the snow for the first time in two years made me a bit nostalgic for my skis.

Since most of our planned events had been wiped out by strikes or floods, we were determined to make the most of the few days remaining on the trailer rental. We headed on south to the city of Dunedin. Dunedin has not shared in the prosperity of the rest of the South Island. There are fewer new glass buildings, more of the quaint old buildings, and a few vacant stores downtown.

Dunedin is quite Scottish by ancestry and spirit. As we walked back from a delicious dinner in the core area of town, we were greeted by a small square ablaze with lights and dancing fountains. A band entertained those assembled. This concluded, a piper struck up on a near balcony and entertained us with several Scottish tunes. We also saw a monument which Emily recognized as a replica of one in Edinburgh, Scotland.

Cruising in the Bay of Islands is worth describing. It was a pastime Sunchaser and Golden Fleece made in tandem on several occasions. A friend of ours, Judy, from Portland, Oregon, replaced Geri as the crew of one for Don, Sunchaser's skipper. Geri had flown home to Florida. The two yachts spent two weeks sailing together and rafted each evening for dinner. Rafting consists of one boat dropping anchor and the other tying alongside.

The Bay of Islands is an area rich in history as it was a favorite stopping place for whalers who ventured into the southern oceans in pursuit of the mighty whales.

We had a guidebook for the bay and each island and bay had a story to tell.

Deep Water Cove, for example, had a fishing camp on it that was much frequented by Zane Grey. Now, only a clear lagoon and a couple of concrete foundations remain. It was just outside this cove that Emily sighted her first blue penguins. Her hours spent on the bowsprit staring at the water searching for these elusive amphibious birds were finally rewarded.

On another island we climbed a steep hill to a former pah. A "pah" is a Maori village that has been fortified and to which the villagers flee when threatened. The pahs were usually located on hills so that the defenders could pelt the attackers with rocks. When the English came with cannons, the shot easily demolished the wooden barricades. Lucky was the chief who could capture a cannon from the British and a cannoneer along with it. This gave him superiority over the nearby tribes who had no such armament.

This particular pah site was blessed with a magnificent view and cursed with the memory of a crazed Maori who threw the son of a white settler off a steep 220-foot cliff that formed one side of the pah. He then murdered his own mother. Eventually, he was hanged. I am still incensed that he is immortalized in a bronze plaque erected at the site. His picture was engraved on the plaque.

Life aboard the Golden Fleece was not all sunshine and sailing. Both Emily and I studied hard and practiced our Morse code so she could get her ham license, and I could up-grade mine. One of the cruising advanced hams from the yacht, Sanctuary, Mike and his crew Ardith, also from Portland, Oregon, organized the classes and many of the cruiser hams either obtained their licenses or up-graded the ones they had. Emily and I didn't advance as far as we wanted, but we are still working on it.

Many of the yachts we cruised with were operated by people who became good friends. Some, with whom we had crossed the Pacific, we didn't see at all in New Zealand because they sought different ports in New Zealand, went on to Australia, stayed in the upper island, or went north to Hawaii.

One of our friends, who elected to go to Hawaii single-handedly, made a slight navigational error and ended up on a reef on a remote uninhabited island where he spent 55 days waiting for rescue.

We had decided to purchase a 32-foot Westsail in Scotland and that decision changed our sailing plans. Golden Fleece was a 28-foot Westsail; her replacement meant more room and convenience. Our decision to buy the Scottish yacht came with difficulty and for several reasons.

Our next cruising objective was the Mediterranean where we planned to spend a year or two. To get there by boat would involve a one-year trip of almost continuous travel with little reward for the cruiser, that is very few interesting and friendly places to visit. The area had a reputation for piracy. The route through the Red Sea and the Suez Canal is rimmed with hostile nations, and the winds are adverse in all but one month of the year. The alternate route around the Cape of Good Hope sends a boat into the stormiest part of the Indian Ocean and a smooth sail around the cape is more a matter of luck than design. After that, there is a long haul up the coast of Africa before you arrive at the gate to the Mediterranean—Gibraltar. So that is why we were glad to learn of this 32-footer for sale in Scotland. Also, ex-American boats for sale in Europe usually sell for about 20 percent less.

We acknowledged that we were giving up part of a dream—to circumnavigate the world. That is what we started out to do, but, well, maybe we will still do it—later.

Parting with the friends we'd made didn't concern us, for we knew sea gypsies would run into one another again. We just knew that we would pull into an anchorage somewhere, some day, and there would be Whalesong and Harry and Marge (or other acquaintances) coming over in their dinghy to welcome us before we could get our anchor down.

Our last month in New Zealand was hectic as we were getting the Golden Fleece ready to ship to the U. S. and to sell. This meant a haul-out to get the hull and bottom painted, a thorough cleaning and varnishing of the interior, and a sanding and oiling of the exterior woodwork.

Another wrenching task was getting rid of accumulated treasures—such as assorted screws, bolts, pieces of wood, short pieces of rope, and odds and ends of things that were too precious yesterday to throw away. Finally, we sailed Golden Fleece down to Auckland, where she was to be put on a container vessel that was soon to load for San Pedro, California.

The week there was full of things to do, but we did go to a couple of shows with Mike and Ardith on Sanctuary and spent an evening celebrating Emily's birthday on an Australian yacht, Luana, with a cake baked especially for the occasion by Debbie, a lovely young teenager.

With Golden Fleece secured tightly to the open container, we bid her goodbye and drove our car to the dealer who had agreed to buy it. We got our money, gave it to the shipping company, and boarded Qantas for Los Angeles.

And, now we are here in Las Vegas visiting my sister and on a long trip to the other side of the world. Will we like our new floating home? What excitement does Europe and the Mediterranean hold? We plan to stop and visit Emily's folks in North Carolina. Darn! I forgot to get her father's permission to marry my 59-year-old bride! He will probably accept me because, when Emily phoned him to tell him of our marriage, he asked, as any good father would, "What does he do?"

Emily replied, "He is a sailor." Since this produced no anguished groans, I probably have a good chance of family acceptance.

I'll write again from Scotland, or somewhere around there. I do like to hear from you all, even if I'm not swift to answer.

Love,
    Paul and Emily

Howth Harbor

7

Dublin,
Ireland
August 21, 1986

Dear Friends,

    Much has happened since our last letter. A change of boat, a change of scene, a change of locale, and a change of pace. The new boat is 32 feet long with two masts, four sails, a diesel engine of 22 horses. There are four bunks with a nice U-shaped galley, navigation table with chest of drawers, and a table that folds out.

    One thing that has not changed is our love of adventure and pursuit of knowledge about the cultures we visit. For example, I have just finished a careful study of Scotch whiskies. We are now in Ireland and we can't decide whether to investigate Irish whiskey or leprechauns. I think Emily will choose the latter (she is already half-way through a volume of Yeats) and the former for me. I have already started on my first case study (brand investigation, not a case of 12).

Our last letter was written as we departed New Zealand and shipped the Golden Fleece by container ship to Los Angeles where it would be sold. We flew home and spent a few days in Las Vegas, the tinsel town of America, with my sister and brother-in-law. The contrast between the quiet challenge of the open seas and the brash neon of the "strip" was hard to reconcile.

We said good-bye to my sister and brother-in-law and flew to Pinehurst, North Carolina and spent a very pleasant 10 days with Emily's family. The words Pinehurst, Golf, and Tufts are almost synonymous. The World Golf Hall of Fame is located there and gives full credit to Emily's grandfather for developing Pinehurst and golf as a sport in this country, and to Emily's uncle for playing a major part in codifying the rules of the game. To do this, he made many visits to St. Andrews, Scotland, the birthplace of golf. Our visit to St. Andrews a couple of weeks ago, therefore, had special significance.

While packing for Scotland, we were sweltering in one of the hottest summers yet in North Carolina. I had carefully put my shorts and light T-shirts on top in my suitcase and had planned to wear them when we arrived in Scotland. Emily suggested it might be a bit cooler there, so I opted for long pants and, for good measure, threw a sweater on top of my carry-on luggage. When we arrived at Prestwick airport, near Glasgow, Emily's foresight was much appreciated in the quite chilly weather that greeted us.

We rented a car and headed for the village on the Gareloch where our possible future floating home lay. There are several things to which we had to adjust—luckily one of them was not having to drive on the wrong side of the road. Remember, in my last letter I said that the New Zealanders were more British than the British. This included driving on the left side of the road. After spending two years in tropical climes, however, we did have to practice dressing more warmly as our skins had grown thinner. The hardy Scots run around in shirt sleeves on days when a sweater and light jacket seemed appropriate for us.

The other adjustment was the language—the Scottish do not speak English! The city of Edinburgh is not pronounced the way it is spelled. It is pronounced "A-din-bruh." You must learn to speak Scottish in Scotland, British in England, and Welsh in Wales. But nowhere is your perfect English understood, except perhaps in Nebraska.

We stopped in Dumbarton, the first night, at a bed and breakfast, and fell into bed. This was our first introduction to bed and breakfasts and it was a delightful experience. The home was an old one, but well maintained and full of antiques. Our bed was comfortable, the breakfast delicious, and the hostess gracious. The next morning we visited the Dumbarton Castle at the suggestion of the hostess and had our first taste of this land that is so rich in history. We then drove on to Rosneath and the shipyard where Isabel, which we renamed Golden Bell after we had concluded its purchase, was sitting forlornly in a huge barn-like building. The boatyard people made us feel welcome and found a fine bed and breakfast nearby for us to stay in while Golden Bell was made ready for sea.

The bed and breakfast was in a 150-year-old stone house standing on the adjacent Loch Long. With a slate roof, a solarium, many massive chimneys with chimney pots on them, a small cliff that included a waterfall, and beyond that a lush meadow complete with cows, provided a lodging that seemed saturated with Scotland's aura. A rustic stone bridge under which ran a "wee" stream beckoned to us. Truly, an enchanting place.

The hostess was a graduate of the Cordon Bleu school in France and a cateress! Her husband was an executive with Ballentyne's distillery in nearby Dumbarton. They loved the house and were proud of its good condition—largely a result of their efforts.

During our short stay there, we were determined to sample as much of the Scottish culture as we were able and one of our outstanding experiences was to attend the Highland Games at Rosneath. This annual event was held in the village of Rosneath on the Gareloch, just off the River Clyde which flows into the Firth of Clyde. At this event, young girls competed for the title of best young dancer in the dancing contest, brawny brutes threw large logs (called a "caber") and heavy weights over bars. Cyclists raced around a track, pipers piped, racers ran, huge hammers were thrown, and a good time was had by all. We were blessed with a rare sunny day and, of course, all were dressed in their kilts and tartans. Aye, 'twas a bonny day we had there.

The Scottish cities we visited had their own charm

and individuality. Many of the homes, including the one in which we were staying, and many commercial and public buildings were listed in the National Registry. This meant that the exterior could not be altered and, if you owned such a building, it must be kept in good shape and repair. It is considered an honor to own and live in one of these buildings and they are much sought after. The central Glasgow area contained many large buildings of this nature, including the city hall which was a large stone pile of awesome massiveness that was liberally sprinkled with gargoyles, statues, turrets, and other ornamentation. It faces on Georges Square which was frequented by the great Scots you and I read about when we studied "English" literature in school. English is in quotes because I quickly learned that England and Scotland are two different countries which, with Wales and Northern Ireland, form the country of Great Britain.

  The capital of Scotland is Edinburgh, a city that permits no growth or change within its limits. The purpose is to prevent the introduction of high-rise building of modern architecture from overwhelming the character that is Edinburgh. A few modern two or three-story glass buildings are present but they were built before the ordinance was passed. Modern glass fronts can be installed by individual stores at their entrances but that is it!

  Emily and I noticed a tower a replica of which we had seen in Dunedin in New Zealand. We learned that it was a monument to Sir Walter Scott. We did not visit it but saw its unmistakable architecture from the castle heights. Everywhere there were charming old buildings, narrow cobblestone streets, archways, long flights of steps, and wrought iron grillwork. Here and there a well-tended flower garden or a cathedral made an appearance. We visited the castle of Edinburgh, official residence of the Duke of Edinburgh, consort to the Queen, and were entranced by it. All that you ever imagined a castle to be was included in Edinburgh. It was on a high rock that dominated the city and contained moats, drawbridges, winding cobblestone roads, and cisterns. On either side of the massive, ornate gate were rooms to house the defending guards. Then you went through more narrow gates that had steel portcullis ready to drop down. Then you went on up to the central part which contained housing for the men-at-arms, officers, court officials, and the royal family. The central compound also contained a chapel, stable, armory, and several other buildings of obscure use. An interesting feature of the design was that all the streets and courtyards were sloped and channeled so that the rains could channel into cisterns—useful in case of siege. We were ushered into a carefully preserved room which was the quarters of Mary Queen of Scots. Also preserved there were the crown, scepter and sword of the Scottish Kingdom. The visit to Edinburgh was an incredible voyage into history.

  Something must be said for St. Andrews, the birth place of golf. There are now numerous courses in the area, but the old original St. Andrews course is still functioning with its venerable old clubhouse. There are golf shops and cafes, most of which have names related to golf. St. Andrews is situated on St. Andrews Bay on the east coast of Scotland. Sand was considered essential to the game in its early days and all courses were laid out on beaches. In back of the beaches strip is the business section of the city and, except for tarmac on the streets, it cannot have changed much in the last two hundred years. There are few, if any, glass fronts and the city square contains the ruins of a 500-year-old church.

Our drive there was through the convoluted countryside, past small stone villages, large baronial estates, across wee streams, and everywhere, we saw fluffy, woolly sheep, beautiful cows, and small stone farm cottages. Scotland is a beautiful storybook land. Unfortunately we were cursed with bad weather, which is also a part of Scotland, and only had three or four bright sunny days in the five weeks we spent there.

We are now on our way to the southern English coast where we will repair, restock, and refurbish Golden Bell. Our new (used) boat is a joy to sail and quite sea kindly. We are already full of plans to make it more livable. The former owner saw it primarily as a vehicle to sail across the ocean with a crew of two or three, and consequently, he built it well, but somewhat starkly. We wanted to turn it into a cozy comfortable home. I, especially have rigging and sailing plans to make it easier and safer to handle.

Many of our grander plans will have to await next winter when we will be holed up somewhere in the Mediterranean, dreaming of the South Pacific, perhaps, where it will then be summer and where many of our friends still are. Another of our problems is that we own two boats, as Golden Fleece has not yet sold. After a week or two on the southern English coast we will cross into France and start our tour through the canals and down to the Mediterranean.

As of this moment we sit in the small harbor of Rosslaire on the bay of Waterford (remember Waterford crystal?) on the south-east corner of Ireland, riding out the worst storm we have yet experienced. The radio promised that we would have force nine winds (just under hurricane force). As I write, we are tied to a rusty fishing boat with nine lines and the fishing boat is tied to the quay with two one-inch hausers. The fishermen are preparing to put another one-incher to the quay. They are recommending that we go ashore and not ride this out in as much as there is a strong possibility that the winds will shift direction and then things will get rougher. We plan to take their advice, button up here, and register in at the local hotel. Incidentally, we think these Irish fishermen are great people.

We really haven't had great breaks with the weather in these British waters. But, then, no one has ever accused Britain of great weather. It will be nice to get into the more southern latitudes and go around in something less than sweaters and windbreakers.

We will write again when we get to France. Until then we hope all goes well with each of you.

    Love,
        Paul and Emily

P.S. It is now the next morning and Golden Bell rode out the storm nicely, but it would have been terrifying had we stayed on board.

BOAT YARD FALMOUTH ENGLAND

8

LeHavre,
France
September 24, 1986

Dear Friends,

    Emily and friend Nancy are off scrounging tires so I will take this chance to bring you up to date. "Scrounging tires?" Yes, that is not an error. Tires are used in trips through the canals to keep the sides of your boat from getting scraped by the rough walls of the locks. Since a lot of boats come across the channel and enter the waterway system at LeHavre it is impossible to find any tires near the harbor. I have this theory that a couple of attractive and helpless females can get a lot more out of a Frenchman than a crusty, bearded old salt.

I left you dangling in our last letter with a hurricane howling in Ireland. As it turned out, Golden Bell did survive very nicely, but when we returned on board, there were several parted lines and those remaining were frayed. Another couple of hours of Hurricane Charlie and the story might have been different.

We remained in Rosslaire for several more days awaiting good weather before we crossed the Irish Sea to Britain. We became rather friendly with the weather professionals at the weather station there. They asked us not to bring any more hurricanes to the British Isles the next time we came and accused us of exporting bad weather. I felt it necessary to point out that Charlie had never touched America having circled past the coast but well out to sea, so it really was anybody's hurricane until it was claimed by Ireland—and would they please greet us with something with a little less gusto the next time we visited them.

On the advice of the pleasant weather professionals, and with the encouragement of the rising barometer, we sailed off to find pirates at Penzance on the southern English coast. We planned for an overnight trip since we had more than 120 miles to go to Land's End, the point of the British Isles that extends the farthest west. It is the usual landfall for transoceanic voyagers heading for Europe. That night we spoke (on the radio) with the chatty captain of a cargo freighter who said that he, too, was going to do as we were doing as soon as he retired in a year or two. He asked us all sorts of questions and left us with a warm glow in our hearts. Not all freighter captains are cruel freebooters whose main purpose in life is to run down small sailboats in the dark of night.

We hit the peninsula too far east not having allowed enough for some navigational factor—drift, leeway, current, compass error—pick one, and this meant that we would round Land's End, not counting the Isles of Scilly, and would pass between those and the mainland late in the evening, possibly after dark. We passed through this "gate" just as dusk fell but had to keep going in the dark using navigation lights as guides.

This ordinarily would have been no great problem but this pass was considered one of the places in the world of heaviest sea traffic concentration. We made it through the straits well on a course for Penzance when I turned the helm over to Emily and answered the call. When I came up on deck a minute later, we were surrounded by freighters and on a course at right angles to the one we should have been on.

Emily was panicked and I was startled also. It didn't seem possible for all those freighters to have sneaked up on us with their lights out. Avoidance tactics were in order and I continued for a short while on a course of 90 degrees from our intended one. The presence of rocks a mile or two to starboard shortened that strategy, so I stopped and waited to see what the freighters were going to do. The two closest had come to a complete halt, one within 100 yards of us. Suddenly a bright spot light was directed at us followed by a statement we clearly heard: "Aw, it's only a small sailboat." Nice to know that you can scare the big fellows even though they make fun of you when they find out who you really are.

Back on course we finally arrived at Newlynn, just

a couple of miles from Penzance, at 2:00 a.m. Tired as we've ever been, we tied to a fisherman and fell into our bunks. The next day we jumped on a Hoppa bus and rode into Penzance looking for pirates. After walking around for a couple of hours and seeing none, but savoring the presence that Gilbert & Sullivan immortalized, we returned to our boat in Newlynn.

The next day was blustery so we stayed in harbor and enjoyed strolling around Newlynn, a picturesque old town with a fine stream running through it crossed by many old stone bridges. There was a lifeboat stationed there and we were able to watch it make a rescue.

A rather foolhardy young man had decided to row to America and had run into foul weather (the same that kept us in port) and had radioed for help. The lifeboat had towed him into port. A word about these lifeboats. The British Coast Guard only guards coastlines. It does not aid mariners in distress. Because of this, a volunteer rescue organization has a proud heritage harking back a couple of centuries.

The lifeboats today are fine vessels containing powerful motors and strong hulls and they are expensive. All have been obtained by subscription and donations both from wealthy people and the general public. It is said that the Queen purchased one boat and donated it to a port whose name I have forgotten. The crews are all volunteers and, of course, proud that they have been chosen.

From Penzance we went on up the coast to Falmouth and, since it was Sunday, threaded our way through a cloud of yachts and carefully navigated up the Fal River to the Falmouth Marina. We spent five days there getting some sail work done and chasing our mail from home.

    The most frustrating experience was trying to negotiate with customs. They had illegally charged us 21 pounds for some parts we had had shipped from the States. The charge was in error because parts shipped to a yacht of U.S. registry were never charged duty. The local postmaster charged us anyhow on the advice of customs and, in typical public servant procedure, he would not release the package with the parts until I had paid the money. I suppose we could have stayed and argued the matter until the fee was reversed, but we were anxious to press on. It was the first of November and we still had to negotiate all of France to reach our winter haven, wherever it was to be.

    Being a stubborn cuss, I did get my money back from the post office after writing a letter to the Chief of Customs in which I said, "the 21 pounds will not greatly enrich Her Majesty's government or impoverish me. It will, however, leave me with a very sour taste in my mouth regarding the people of Britain, and Her Majesty's customs officials." A week later a check arrived in the mail. So you see, government inertia can be overcome!

    My visit to Falmouth was memorable for another reason. It was the home port of Captain (later Lord) Horatio Hornblower—my hero! I had been introduced to him through the books of C. S. Forrester about a year earlier and had eagerly devoured every volume I could find. I strolled casually past the Admiral's House where Hornblower had played such a masterful game of whist frequently earning more money at the game than his salary as a shorebound naval officer. I posed for a photograph in front of the Hornblower Restaurant and noted the piers of ancient vintage where his water barges took on water to deliver to his ships. It is not often that one can stand in the vicinity of greatness, even if the reflected glory comes from a fictional character.

Next we went up to Plymouth, at the mouth of the Ply River, and saw the same steps down which the pilgrims descended to board their boat for the New World. There is very little of the old city left. Plymouth was the main British naval base during World War II and was bombed into rubble by the Germans early in the war. There still exists, however, the bowling green where Sir Francis Drake was playing when the great Spanish Armada was sighted approaching the harbor. When asked, "What are we going to do?" he replied, "First I will finish my game of bowls."

This coolness greatly impressed the British people, but was, in fact, based on a thorough knowledge of the facts. His ships, based in Plymouth, could not exit the harbor until the tide changed in about two hours. In the meantime, none of the Spanish ships dared approach too closely because of the shore batteries. After finishing the bowls game, Drake sipped some refreshments and casually boarded his gig to go out to his flagship. The story from there is well known. He sailed out into the channel, trounced the mightiest armada of ships ever assembled in those days, and chased the remnant into the North Sea where it was surrendered. Spain never rose from that defeat and lost its dominance as a sea power.

We moved on to Dartmouth appropriately enough at the mouth of the Dart River. This river and town are difficult to observe from the sea unless you are quite close. We crept closer and closer and finally hailed a passing sailboat for directions. It looked to us as though we were approaching a sheer rock cliff and the water was getting shallower and shallower. We were advised to go right ahead until we saw the "Castle." "Are we on a good course?" I asked the sailboat skipper.

"Yes, a fine course,." he replied.

It takes courage to sail straight into a sheer rock wall, but we trusted our anonymous friend and sailed on. When we were about 500 yards from the cliff, we could see a small stone building sort of standing out. This we hoped was the castle and kept on our course. When we were within two hundred yards of the "castle" things began to open up and suddenly there was a river flowing out at an angle that made an approach from our direction seem to be heading into a sheer rock face.

Dartmouth is a charming city and we found the port officials and customs most helpful. We would have liked to stay there longer, but we prepared to cross the channel from there cancelling our original plan to go on up to the Isle of Wight before crossing.

Our stay at Dartmouth was memorable because of a rude waiter who refused to take away our dishes after we had finished eating our meal. He informed us haughtily that we had not placed our fork and knife in the proper position on the plate. He then showed us how to place them in the future so that we would not have to sit unattended with our forks signaling the waiter that we had not concluded our meal. He never approached us for any reason although we sat at our table for ten minutes doing nothing. I think he just didn't like heterosexual people.

We stocked up on groceries and beverages, obtaining spirits from bonded dealers at a greatly reduced rate on the basis that we were exiting the country. A customs official came aboard and sealed one of the compartments in which the spirits were stored and with strict, but friendly instructions, told us not to open it until we were three miles off-shore.

On the fourth day we were in Dartmouth, the harbormaster came out to our boat and told us that the French had just closed their borders to all foreigners without visas and that visas would have to have been obtained in your home country before you left it. He telephoned London and talked with the French consul who assured him that if we left within the next two weeks we would be granted a three-month tourist visa when we entered.

I looked at Emily and said, "Let's go!" At 10:30 p.m. we set out to cross the English Channel, one of the busiest shipping routes in the world. Another reason we decided to leave was because one of Emily's best friends, Nancy, was in Holland and had planned to visit us on the boat. We called her and said, "Meet us in LeHavre in two days." This meant that she could enjoy the trip up the Seine instead of the unexciting sail across the channel. As it turned out, it wasn't really all that boring.

We were threatened very little by the shipping in the channel even though we saw the running lights of many ships. During the next day, we passed close to Cherbourg and identified the Balfour light just as dusk came. We estimated that we would arrive off LeHavre about dawn.

We actually arrived about 3:00 a.m. just as a thick fog settled in. We knew our approximate location, so when we chanced on a buoy we decided to stay close to it until the fog lifted. For six more hours. we circled the buoy making certain that we were not drifting into the beach or out into the busy shipping lanes. At 8:00 a.m. we called the harbormaster in LeHavre, who, in rather good English, told us to just stay where we were and the fog would lift about 10:00 a.m. At 9:00 a.m. the fog had thinned enough so that we could see the buoys on the dredged entrance channel about one-half mile away, although the city was not yet visible. We could also see several freighters which had anchored near our buoy. We were glad that we had hugged the buoy and that none of those huge brutes had dropped anchor on our little boat. By 10:00 a.m. we were in the harbor and a launch came out to lead us into the marina.

A courteous customs man came down to our boat and checked us into France—for 90 days only. I felt a bit irked by this. Their reason for closing the borders was because of the terrorists who had exploded some bombs in Paris. Yet all members of the European Community were free to come and go at will—including Germans who had twice invaded France in this century, and both time the U.S. had helped rescue them from their oppressors. And now we were unwelcome. Ah, 'tis the way of politics!

Nancy, our expected guest, arrived and found us at the marina, and, as I write, is out scrounging tires with Emily. More about that later.

I'll get this off to the States quickly as we won't have much time to spare until we get to Paris.

    Fair winds,
        Paul and Emily

9

Diou,
France
November 10, 1986

Dear Friends,

We are now about halfway through the canals of France and are obliged to layover for two days while the canal at our location is being repaired. It seems like a good time to write to my friends. A canal, of course, is a watery highway for business and pleasure, but, unlike highways on land, there is no way a detour can be easily arranged. So when the canals are closed, you just wait. The French are very good about informing you ahead of time about construction and closures. In fact a bulletin can be obtained from the canal department that lists scheduled closures up to a year in advance. Diou is a charming little town with vegetable gardens and we are moored alongside of them. The colorful plots are painstakingly cared for by the local residents who live just a short walk away.

I mentioned in our last letter from LeHavre that Emily and her friend, Nancy, had gone ashore to scrounge for rubber tires and we needed them because they are used as bumpers to keep the boat and its woodwork away from the rough walls of the locks. Emily and Nancy returned in a taxi with six tires they had found in various gasoline stations. Their jovial taxi driver obviously had enjoyed driving the women on their errands. He had found stations for them and negotiated with the owners. Emily and Nancy both spoke French but in a limited sense. Nancy, a geneticist at Oregon Health Sciences University, had given a paper at a conference in Holland a few days earlier and was now unwinding with her long-time friend. The two girls (I know they are older women but when they returned they were acting like girls!) were quite proud of their accomplishment—and deserved to be. The grinning taxi driver helped unload his trunk full of tires onto the dock.

When we were in Falmouth, a local sail-maker had given us an old, torn canvas sail to use as a skirt to protect the sides of the boat from the marks of the tires hanging over the sides. We divided the sail and gave half to Dick and Bev of the yacht Balena nearby cruisers like ourselves. Now we were ready to make use of our half-sail for Golden Bell. We draped three-foot strips of the sailcloth around the sides of Golden Bell and then hung the tires from the railings. We looked strange but were prepared to take on any lock.

While we were getting the tires in place, we were visited by a chap from an English yacht down at the end of the pier. He had no chart, no compass, and had just crossed the English Channel with his wife who had a leg problem and was unable to walk! I didn't know whether to classify him as brave or stupid. But he wanted to follow us to the entrance of the Seine, as he had no chart. Once in the Seine, he anticipated no problems going across France in the canals. Of course, I agreed, telling him that we were going to leave at 0900 in order to catch the tidal bore.

In the tidal portion of the Seine (or any river for that matter), when the tide is flowing out, the current is much stronger than the normal flow of the river. When the tide is flowing in, the current is much slower than normal and may actually flow upriver. Obviously, this is the best time to travel upriver—particularly when you have a slow boat. The next day with our friend following, we motored out of the harbor into the bay and traveled over to the entrance of the Seine River, about six kilometers away. We glanced back occasionally to see if the Englishman and his wife were staying with us. I told him he could follow us if he could maintain five knots.

Soon after we passed by Honfleur, well inside the river, we lost them, we having been boarded by the French customs boat which stopped our progress for a while. We didn't see the English boat again until we reached Rouen. We discovered they had developed engine trouble and the same customs boat that had boarded us, towed them into Honfleur. They lived on the Island of Ibiza, one of the Balearics, off the east coast of Spain. They had bought their boat in England and were taking it home. They were a cute couple, but we worried about them and hoped they would make their journey without more trouble.

One of the joys of the cruising life is the people you meet. We have met authors, teachers, doctors, engineers, scientists, lawyers, psychologists, even an opera singer who kept his tuxedo pressed and on board in case he had a chance along the way to earn a few bucks. We also met a man with a royal title, a real, live Earl. He obtained his title the hard way, by buying it. We met him in Rouen where he was tied up just astern of us.

He was a contractor who specialized in restoring old buildings. A piece of property he purchased had a title connected to it. He planned to make a bundle restoring the castle and then selling it and the title to some rich American. Now, that's an entrepreneur!

Traveling through France on the rivers is totally different from traveling in the canals. The canals are serene, tranquil, and completely bucolic. The rivers, on the other hand, are busy. On the Seine, at least as far as Rouen, there are giant ocean liners, many peniches (the small 100 x 20 foot motorized barges), some pleasure boats, and large bulk-cargo barges. The river is lined with small villages, picturesque villas, some with thatched roofs, and ancient castles, one of which was the castle of Richard the Lion Hearted.

An amusing incident occurred when Nancy and Emily went to Vernon, a little way up the river from Rouen. They decided to take the train and dutifully read the timetable. Arriving at the station at 7:00 a.m. they boarded the train, settled in their seats and prepared to watch the river go by, which it did with amazing rapidity. They knew that something was wrong when the conductor announced their arrival in Paris. They had boarded the 7:00 a.m. express because we had not set our clocks back from Daylight Savings Time to Standard Time. Their train to Vernon did not leave for another hour. A kindly and amused conductor in the Paris station allowed them to board the return on the local train without charge. They got off at Vernon, walked to Giverny, the actual location of Monet's home, and worshiped at the house of the master. They even dangled their fingers in the water of the famous lily ponds.

I could write a book about Rouen and tell about its famous cathedral, its bustling economy, and its museums and quaint streets and shops. The cathedral is huge and the facades of the various entrances are so elaborately decorated with stone carvings as to defy description. Its turrets soar to the skies on the backs of statues of angels and figures from the Bible. You admire this with sadness because acid rain is taking its toll and you know that unless something is done, your children's children will have only photographs to illustrate the grandeur that once existed. Unfortunately, we saw no evidence that protective measures were being taken.

Another of the delights of Rouen was the Museum of St. Joan d'Arc. The building itself is very modernistic and looks a little out of place surrounded by half-timbered houses and cafes in old buildings. I did not go in but Nancy and Emily did and were impressed not only by the exhibits but by the way in which they were displayed and the aura of the interior. There, too, in the square I ate my first (and last) escargot. I agreed to do this after being needled by Emily and Nancy. What was a guy to do? As far as I know, no one has ever died from eating escargot. My impression?

Small strips of leather, deep fried, and dipped in a heavy garlic sauce, then swallowed whole and as quickly as possible.

We left Rouen and Nancy, who returned the U. S. After saying good-bye to Nancy and to our acquaintances the Earl and the English couple who had finally arrived in Rouen after making repairs in Honfleur, we proceeded upstream. We left all of the large vessels behind and had only peniches and pleasure boats to share the river with. We stopped at Vernon where the remains of an old Roman bridge still exist, now replaced by a modern structure. We stood on that bridge and took a picture of it and Golden Bell. The photograph is one of pure rural tranquility, but only the photographer knows that behind him is a quintessential modern town.

Coming into Paris was an exciting experience. The river approaches were lined almost completely with factories, yards, and other depressing (but necessary) sights. Soon these gave way to dwellings and this ushered in the procession of bridges.

Ah, the bridges of Paris! Magnificent, each one. Ornate statues, pillars, and decorations made each one a work of art. Traffic, especially pleasure traffic, including tour boats, became heavier and, fortunately was regulated. Our guidebook had a picture of each bridge, and named it, and showed which arch we passed under. The guidebooks we had, Les Carte Guide Navigation Fluviales, were very well done and contained everything we needed to know. We had them for all the canals and rivers we expected to travel.

We passed a perfect replica of the Statue of Liberty and not far beyond we found our objective, the Port de

Plaisance at the Basin de L'Arsenal. It wasn't easy. The marina is in a little-used canal and you must lock up into it. We knew we were in the exact spot according to the guide, but all we saw was a bridge, heavy with traffic, a slight indentation in the shoreline, buttressed with a wall, and a small landing. Went to the landing, tied up and there was a squawk-box communicator on a post.

I pressed the button and a totally garbled voice issued forth, in French, of course. I answered slowly in English and stated our mission. He answered in English but with a heavy accent. That, combined with the acoustical unintelligibility of the device, required several repetitions before we understood that we were just to go in. I climbed back on Golden Bell and Emily cast off. There had been a change. The wall buttress had swung aside and there was a narrow stone box in its place. Aha! Our first lock. We entered and a loudspeaker and green lights were there to encourage us and guide us. Soon the lock filled and we were presented with a rather large basin with an official-looking building at its end and lots of boats! We motored over to a landing where there were many people with cameras.

A handsome young Frenchman who spoke very good English welcomed us and jumped aboard to take us to our moorage position. He informed us that we had just barged in on a television drama being filmed and that it didn't include the arrival of a salty American boat with two masts laying on it. An hour later we learned that the photographers on the landing were waiting the arrival of a sleek motor cruiser with elegantly gowned people aboard. To this day, Emily still swoons when she thinks of that handsome young officer jumping aboard our boat.

In the two weeks we were at Port de Plaisance (Port de Plaisance translates as "port for pleasure boats" or "marina" in the U.S.), we sampled as much of memorable Paris as we could. We learned to ride the Paris Metro, we visited some of the sights, and museums, strolled along the Champs -Elysées and did a lot of the things other tourists do. We never visited the Eiffel Tower, although it was visible and taunting us most of the time. The highlights of our visit were several. One of our most beautiful experiences occurred when we visited the Sainte Chapelle on the Isle de la Cité. We toured this beautiful, colorful chapel during the afternoon.

A guide suggested that a night visit would be a totally different experience. We noted that a concert was being held there that evening. The afternoon experience was dominated by the magnificent stained-glass windows that radiated glorious patterns and colors. In the evening, the colors of the enamels illuminated by the sparkling chandeliers were almost breathtaking. The addition of Mozart from a fine string orchestra completed this enchanting sensual feast.

The Louvre is, of course, famous as one of the outstanding art museums in the world. To stroll its many corridors and galleries is a privilege. The flowing stone lines of "Winged Victory," the magnificent "Venus de Milo," the world's best known painting "Mona Lisa", all were there and were living proof that all I had read about in Art 101 was true. Later, we strolled down the Champs Elysées and found a sidewalk cafe where we had a Campari as the sun sank behind the Arc de Triomphe, and then grabbed the Metro back to the Basin d'Arsenal.

Our enjoyment of that day and others was

somewhat dampened by the presence of pairs of uniformed soldiers patrolling the streets with their sub-machine guns slung over their shoulders. Also, when we entered stores, a guard at the door searched all handbags. These precautions were the result of a recent outbreak of terrorist incidents. In the marina, we removed our U.S. flag for the same reason.

What can you say about Paris? Paris is Paris. There is no other city like it to my knowledge, and there will never be another. Lest you get the wrong idea, we think it is a great place to visit, but we wouldn't want to live there. The taxi drivers are rude, the streets are confusing with little organization, the citizens are not friendly nor helpful. They do not encourage your halting French; they just turn away. The waiters are all very nice—but they are paid to be. We have since learned that there are two Frances—Paris, and the rest of France. The country people are friendly, smiling, and helpful. But Paris is Paris and not to be missed.

We enjoyed the company of Dick and Bev on Balena, who came into the basin a couple of days after we did. They planned to spend the winter in Paris, except for a couple of months visiting in the U.S., and then do the canals in the spring. Our English couple popped in briefly for a day or two and then headed on up the river ahead of us. We felt that since they had progressed as far as they had, we could stop worrying about them.

One of the great rewards of cruising life is to meet people like Dick and Bev who share your interests. Both were inclined toward the arts and, like Emily, had talent along those lines. We visited a number of museums in their company and enjoyed every moment of it. We also made the acquaintance of Hal and Dorothy of the boat

Pennsylvania Yankee. Pennsylvania Yankee is an English narrowboat, eight feet wide and about 30 feet long, designed for negotiating the narrow British canals. On the basic barge, Hal had mounted a superstructure that resembled a travel trailer, gaily painted and divided into useful compartments. In the back was a small deck which served as the location of the steering equipment. The barge did not sail and we anxiously asked Hal if he had driven it across the channel. He said, "Yes, on a trailer, on a ferry." But it was an ideal boat for cruising the canals.

We continued on up the Seine in company with Pennsylvania Yankee. Our engine was a little more powerful than the one on the Yankee so we had to throttle back to avoid overtaking and passing them. We arrived at the first lock only to find that the lockkeeper was on strike. We moored in the entrance of one of two locks which was supposed to be out of order. We were joined by Hal and Dorothy for dinner. Hal was an enthusiastic ham radio operator and every evening would go out and string wire to points on the shore to enable him to contact friends, mostly in England. Dorothy is a pizza specialist and the next night performed admirably for our benefit. My stomach groaned a bit at the extra load it was required to carry. We enjoyed our journey with Hal and Dorothy.

The next day we were awakened at 7:00 a.m. by the lockkeeper who wanted us to get out of the broken lock entrance. Of course, it wasn't out of order as we had been told. The lockkeeper planned to use both locks to process the accumulated peniches and pleasure boats stacked up by the strike. We dutifully moved aside and he filled the lock with peniches but there was enough space left for us so we hurried in.

If I have to criticize the French people for anything, it is the stoic manner with which they accept the frequency of strikes. Our little wildcat strike was caused by a union which claimed membership from only one in five of the lockkeepers. The peniche operators, when asked, were unable to tell us why they were striking, nor did they seem to care that their schedule had been set back a day. "C'est un greve" (It is a strike), they said with a Gallic shrug of their shoulders, as if to say, "Who knows and who cares. It is the way of things and we must accept it." To this pugnacious American, that rankled.

At St. Mammes, we said goodbye to the Pennsylvania Yankee, as Hal and Dorothy were going on up the Seine for a few more days and would then put their boat up for the winter at Auxerre, a town where they had placed it the previous year. It was easy, apparently, to haul it out there and the area was well guarded and not too expensive. At this point, we left the Seine and entered the Canal du Centre. It was late in the afternoon when we traversed two close locks and moored beside the canal just above them still in the city of St. Mammes.

We soon settled into a routine in the canal system. First a leisurely breakfast, then cast off and proceed along our way. Each day consisted of our studying the charts, determining the number of locks we had to negotiate in the next six or seven hours, and perhaps selecting a target town based on our guidebook's description. The locks in the canals were smaller and more frequent than in the rivers, and they were only big enough to hold one peniche. In the river locks, as many as six peniches could be handled, as well as a few pleasure boats.

Chugging through the locks got to be routine. The

lockkeeper opened the lower gate if the lock was empty. If full we waited until the vessel in the lock emerged into the canal after having been lowered. Then it was our turn and we entered the lock. Emily then climbed the wet and slimy ladder set into the wall, carrying a mooring line which she looped over a bollard (a very sturdy post set in concrete). I then tossed her the stern line which she looped over another bollard.

Next, she walked back and operated the gate mechanism to close the rear gates. The eclusier (lockkeeper) operated the one on the other side of the lock. The water entered and raised Golden Bell to the top. Emily, in the meantime got to practice her French on the eclusier, gave him a two-franc tip, scuttled forward to the forward gate and opened it. The eclusier opened the other gate. Emily untied the lines, stepped aboard and we proceeded slowly out into the canal. My job, as captain, while she got all the exercise, was to steer the boat. We then proceeded to the next lock which might be half a kilometer away or as many as six.

We had one interesting adventure for which I as captain claimed full (ignominious) credit. The chart indicated a halte de plaisance (stop for pleasure boats) two hundred or so meters up a river. We ducked under a bridge and proceeded up the river and encountered a large sign that warned the maximum depth of water at the pier was one meter. We drew only 1.5 meters. I don't usually have a problem with simple math, but this time my circuits got shorted. I blithely approached the float and went hard aground. I mean <u>hard</u>! As I maneuvered to get off, I only succeeded in getting us further aground.

A Frenchman who lived alongside the river came

out in his small outboard to render assistance. (He was a country Frenchman, not a Paris Frenchman.) He took our long spare anchor line across the river and tied it to a tree. My idea was to winch us off, but it didn't work. The Frenchman, who spoke good British- accented English, told us that we should not worry, he would tell the chief of the pompier (the fire department) and the next morning they would get us off. We were having breakfast the next morning when we noticed eight young men dressed in uniform were standing on the float laughing and smoking.

Soon our French friend appeared and said the chief would be along in a few minutes in a boat. The chief arrived and asked if we had a strong line. I showed him the anchor line and said that we had 100 meters of it. At his point, he barked orders to the young men on the float and they walked downstream along the shore. He took the end of the line ashore in his boat and the eight young huskys grabbed hold of it. The chief hooked a small line to our boat, positioned his boat downstream and with a shout to the men on shore we began to move. Bump! jar! grind! crunch! and we were off. We dropped the anchor, retrieved our line, and with a profusion of thanks to everyone were off down the river and back into the canal. As we passed under the bridge Emily asked, "Why did you think you could get to that pier when we draw 1.5 meters?" It suddenly dawned on me what I had done, and I didn't want to talk about it any more.

The canals are beautiful and as we traveled the ribbon of water, we passed neat farms growing corn. We didn't see any vineyards as this was not wine country. The banks were lined with trees, frequently a planted row of lombardy poplars. They were beginning to turn to fall colors and I shot several rolls of film trying to capture their beauty.

Sometimes we passed through small villages and it was evident that their past glory and raison d'etre was the canal. Sometimes we stopped and found the local patisserie and purchased some of that wonderful French bread. We also saw a lot of cattle, almost exclusively the Charolais, those white-coated cattle that produce such good milk and cheese and are also excellent for meat. We occasionally met a peniche and this was usually traumatic.

The canals were designed to accommodate these motorized, live-aboard barges and the locks held only one at a time. The canals were wide enough for two to pass, but they had to go very slowly. The peniches approaching us often slowed down, but only a little, and some of them, probably captained by former Paris taxi drivers, didn't slow at all. When that happened, their turbulence made it extremely difficult to control our boat. We bent a trim tab on our rudder when the first taxi-jockey passed us.

One other experience that bears noting was our crossing of the Eiffel Bridge. It was designed by the same man who designed the Eiffel Tower. It is a magnificent bridge. There were only two ways we could cross the bridge. On foot or by boat—yes, by boat! Our canal crossed the Loire River on the Eiffel Bridge. The bridge replaced a number of locks that would have meant locking down into the valley and up again on the other side after crossing the river.

We were confused as we paused before the entrance to the bridge, in as much as there before us was a ribbon of water, just a little wider than our boat. The traffic rules we thought were on a brass plate, but the French was beyond our understanding. The only thing we understood was "blow your horn." That we did and then entered the bridge. Emily wanted to go slow, I wanted to go fast in order to reach the other side before a large peniche turned the corner, entered the bridge and disputed the right-of-way with us. Well, we made the one kilometer in short order and no one appeared at the other end. In fact, we didn't see a peniche all that day. It was the first time I have ever stood on a boat and looked <u>down</u> 100 feet to the river.

We probably won't write again until we arrive in Barcelona, a couple of months from now, but that doesn't mean that we won't be thinking of you. Keep well and happy.

Love,
　　　Paul and Emily

View from Galley Port
Sête

10

Valras-Plage,
France
January 4, 1987

Dear Friends,

    We are now on the southwestern coast of France. This area is not as posh as the French Riviera, but it is pretty nice. It has developed more slowly than the eastern coast because it is in the path of the mistral. The mistral is a strong wind that blows from the northwest and across the narrow stretch of land that connects France with Spain. Mistrals are sort of funnelled by the Pyrenees out onto the Golfe du Lion but the Alps divert them from the French

Riviera. We are now pinned down for a day or two to give the cold, dry winds a chance to blow out.

When I last reported from Diou, we still had two mountains to climb, a valley to cross, and a slide down two rivers to the sea. Taking your boat through canal locks down stream is a breeze compared to locking up. The latter is all we had done it seemed from the time we left Paris. Typically, the procedure we developed to lock down was to motor into the lock, which appeared to be nothing more than a quiet pool with a square edge around it. Emily would step down to the edge and walk back to the operating mechanism. Then she and the eclusier shut the entry gates. Silently and smoothly the water flowed out and your boat would sink into a big, square stone hole. The doors would open in front of us and we would motor out into the serenity of the canal.

We ascended the Loing Valley, descended into the Loire Valley, ascended to the Saône Valley and descended to the Saône River. Down the Saône to the Rhône, the Rhône to the Petit Rhône, then laterally through the swampy southern coast to Sete.

We left Sète a few days ago and are getting a little desperate having progressed only slightly toward our destination of Barcelona since erecting the masts and sailing out into the Mediterranean. We could have crossed the country by air in two hours, by France's TGV (fast-t) train in two days. It took us three months and were it not for delays, we could have done it in two.

While we traveled through the canals and river systems of France, we moved every day we could. Strikes, foul weather, or mechanical problems often delayed us. Occasionally we took a day off for sight-seeing or just to rest. Twenty-two locks were the highest number we completed in one day.

On one eventful Sunday we went through some marshy country. The sound of shotguns filled the air and so did lead pellets. We hunkered down in the cockpit and prayed. The French are great lovers of fishing and hunting. The canals were lined with fishermen who would usually wave as we went by. A few gazed intently at their bobbers as we passed them and did not take note of us. The sight of a hunter with his dogs in the fields was common. In England we saw a lot of fat, unhealthy dogs. In France we saw only healthy, active dogs—most of them hunters.

Our night moorages were sometimes at the halte plaisances, where we would often find electricity (220 volts), water, and sometimes showers. In many of the villages, the town fathers had provided a floating dock to which two or three pleasure boats could tie. These were a concession to the many pleasure boats that ply up and down these canals during the summer and were called "Halte Plaisance."

We enjoyed most the times we tied to trees out in the countryside or drove mooring stakes into the ground to hold us to the wall of the canal.

We recall the night we spent with the cows with considerable nostalgia. We were approaching a small town which, purportedly, had a quay to which we could secure, when we sighted a tranquil country scene. There was a pasture, a stone barn, a small farmhouse, trees, including a weeping willow, lots of grass and a herd of five Charolais.

Emily said, "What a lovely scene. Let's spend the night here." The only jarring note was when a peniche went roaring by and almost upset our supper. Our lines held and we spent a tranquil night. Our bovine friends were there as we retired and were still there in the morning. I like to think that they kept the tigers away during the night. To recall this night we have only to say, "Do you remember the night we spent with the cows?"

One other vivid Halte was our meeting with the girl from Texas. We had pulled into a rather dingy quay in the commercial area at the village of Saint Satur. I had just returned aboard when we heard a woman's voice call, "Hi, where ya'll from?" I turned to see a spectacular blond of sturdy build wearing high black boots and a tartan cape. She turned out to be, after introductions, Ann from Texas.

On her way home from her job, she had seen our American flag. Within minutes we were in her Jeep on the way to the local supermarket. We learned all about her and she about us. She was the daughter of a civil employee of the U.S. Armed Forces in Germany who had decided to retire in this area of France and had bought a small farm. Ann was rehabilitating and remodeling it for her mother.

She was also a disc jockey on the local radio station where she had been hired for two hours in the morning to play American pop music. Of course she spoke French fluently and was of great help to us as we shopped. She invited us to visit the famous village nearby whose wine is the world-renowned Sancerre. The village of Sancerre, we discovered as she drove, is on a hill. After a tour of the village, we accompanied her to a local cave where we sampled some of Sancerre's best stored in the dark cavern. We visited Ann's mother's house and then Ann returned us to our boat.

The next morning, she brought her French boyfriend down to see us as we had promised to help them evaluate a boat that they were considering buying. This we did and spent a pleasant hour with them. Ann had to go to her job at the radio station and suggested we tune in as we left. We were hardly out of the marina, where we had moved for fuel, when we heard her come on. We also heard her say, "Bon voyage à mes amis sur le bateau Americain" (A good voyage to my friends on the American boat.).

About this time I started to have some painful back problems. Standing still and erect and steering with only slight movements of the tiller was causing cramps. When I was an usher at a theater in college, I had experienced the same cramps because I was forced to stand motionless for long periods. We called those "ushers' cramps." The ones I had on the boat should have been designated "canal cramps." Relief was obtained by putting one leg up on a stool or something and shifting to the other leg about every 10 minutes. And, of course, Emily relieved me at the helm so I could walk around.

As we approached Nevers, we were forced to wait a short time while a peniche and a plaisance (pleasure boat) were processed through a double lock. In a double lock we entered the lower one, were raised, and then moved right into the next lock where we were raised again. The plaisance turned out to be a 20-foot sailboat from England with a middle-aged man and a bubbly teenager aboard. They had broken their mast in a lock and were returning to Paris to have it repaired. We locked up and there before us was a bridge that crossed a tributary of the Loire. It was quite an experience to lock up and then cross a bridge. The bridge was utilitarian and did not approach the grandeur or size of the Eiffel Bridge.

Canal courtesy is nothing more than treating others

as you would like to be treated. We tried to think as though we were lockkeepers and peniche operators. Most of the eclusiers (lockkeepers) were friendly and helpful. Only a few were surly and uncooperative. Emily, demure and shy, yet always trying to communicate and to practice her French, touched everyone. No one but the hardest of hearts could resist her. Her smile and the two-franc tip, which we never failed to offer, seemed to smooth our way and we never had to wait for more than a few minutes for a lock to open. Frequently it would open as we approached.

Contrasted with the treatment we received, was a British couple who were quite upset with the eclusiers. The wife was a haughty, but nice person and informed us that they never gave a tip unless they got very good service. They waited from 15 minutes up to two hours at empty locks before they were admitted. The eclusiers are linked by radio and I suspect their opinions of boaters are transmitted along with the fact that they are passing a craft to the next lock. We discovered that they do really appreciate your advising them when you are planning to stop so that the next eclusier does not have to wait for you to arrive, perhaps past his quitting time.

By now we were occasionally finding frost and ice on the decks in the morning. The cold days were also clear days and each frost heightened the color of the trees. We were racing (at five miles per hour) the sun to the warm Spanish coast. We stopped at a marina in a small town for the night and spoke with a Dutch boat (all Dutch people seem to speak excellent English). They were spending the winter there, as they had done the previous year because the wife had good friends in the town. The husband was not pleased with the prospect of staying in the pool in which our boats floated. It had grown four inches of ice the year before.

We were now running into automatic locks, a good design idea when they work properly. They operate with an electric eye system that opens and closes the gates and raises and lowers water levels.

We came to one stretch of five locks that were all manned by one lockkeeper. We discovered from the eclusier, who arrived in a great cloud of dust, that the automatic functioning of the gates had gone bad. In his small white French car, he had to scurry back and forth operating the locks by hand. He was apologetic and said the automatic locks had never worked properly. He wished for the old days. We became good friends as he drove down to the next four locks to assist us on our way.

We did a lot of lock-ups and lock-downs in the next few days and finally reached the deepest of them all, an awesome 15 meters (nearly 50 feet). From that one, we entered the Saône River and began our descent to the sea.

It was in the Saône that we had one adventure with good and bad aspects. Our motor failed and we had to buy a new one. That was the bad part. The good part was that we met Jacqueline and Pierre and their son, Ives. The story starts when our motor began to give us trouble. We stopped at a modest town and found a diesel mechanic who worked mostly on cars, but agreed to come and look at our motor. With the motor apparently repaired after his attention, we headed out for Mâcon, farther downstream. Suddenly the motor started stuttering again. We limped back. The same mechanic came, got things running again, and we started out only to have a repeat breakdown about four kilometers down the river. We elected to limp onto Mâcon, a much larger town, and we tied up at the marina. The friendly harbormaster was helpful directing us to a qualified Volvo mechanic, a transplanted German named M. Stuche. After tearing the engine apart he said mournfully, "Seh mock." Emily was unable to translate his French but we persisted until a young man strolled over and translated for us.

"It is dead," he said.

"Oh", said Emily. "That is what he was saying, it is dead. C'est mort."

"Yes", said the nice young man, "but his French is terrible. I will stay here and help if I can."

So we found out via Ives that the bearings were bad, the pistons were shot, and the injectors were old. We asked the German for an estimate to repair the engine. The next day he returned with the figures and suggested that we go to the nearby small city of Chalon sur Saône and price a new motor. The difference between buying a new motor and repairing the old one was less than $1,000, we discovered. The Volvo dealer did not have one in stock, but assured me that when it arrived we could just take out the old one and drop in the new one. This did not turn out to be true, and had I known it, I would have ordered a more powerful three cylinder version. As it was, M. Stuche finally got it installed on a very cold day and we were able to continue on down the Saône.

We invited Ives for coffee and he casually announced that his mother would come by soon and invite us to their house for tea. She, whose name was Jacquelene, did and we were driven in her car to their home. It was a modest house on a lane in a nice residential area, decorated with some fine painting, excellent sculptures, some interesting furniture of ornate design, and other works of art. We learned that all of it had been done by her husband, Pierre, who had just retired as a teacher of art at the local university. We enjoyed the tea and several other people whom we met who had gathered for the cocktail hour.

When the other guests left Jacquelene invited us to stay and have soup with them. We saw much of them during the next few days and some of the most amusing experiences were the conversations that occurred between Emily and Jacquelene. Emily, anxious to improve her French and having found a sympathetic soul in Jacquelene, would address her statements in French. Jacquelene would reply in English, as she was equally determined to improve her speaking ability in our native tongue. Pierre and I would sit in the front seat and say little as he knew little, if any, English, and I knew less French. He was a man of great talent and she was a very gracious woman. It was a privilege to have met them.

When we left Mâçon we encountered fog and were unable to travel far. We attempted to move convinced the fog would dissipate, then were trapped out on the river when it didn't. An American yacht passed us during a break in the fog. The occupants were from Denver, Colorado and soon disappeared in a fog bank farther down the river. We wondered what they knew that we didn't about navigating in the fog. Apparently nothing because soon they reappeared and tied near us in an old abandoned lock. We sat in the sun, having lunch with them and glaring at the fog bank below us.

The fog finally cleared and we went on into Lyon where the Saône joins the Rhône. We arrived early so we explored the town on foot. It is a modern town with a mixture of historic buildings that is pleasing. My one mission in the town was to find some peanut butter. Apparently the French do not eat it. At last we found someone who understood us when we asked for pate de cacahouette. He led us to a natural food store—that was closed. The next morning before we got underway, I trudged into the store and purchased a half-kilo of peanut butter. Some things are worth going the extra mile. We also had had our mail sent there, which we got, and also purchased a few traveler's checks at the American Express office.

The lower Rhône has a fearsome reputation, largely based on the time 20 to 30 years ago when the river was without dams to control it. Now there are many dams, the river has been tamed, and canals bypass rapids that used to strike terror in the hearts of small boatmen heading down or struggling up the river. A pilot was required for all craft, which would have made the Rhône portion of such a journey as ours rather expensive. Now the river has been harnessed and the dams generate electricity in addition to slowing down the river. There are frequent locks to negotiate including some whoppers. We fell in with two other yachts from Britain and traveled in concert as far as Avignon. They suggested that the lockkeepers were reluctant to accommodate only one small yacht. We had not experienced any such reluctance in the locks so far, but did welcome their companionship.

We arrived in Avignon after dark in company with our companions and tied to a historic quay after a particularly long day. The next day, we assumed our tourist role and explored this ancient and historic city. Large portions of the ancient walls are still in existence, including the ornate south entrance. This was the capital of Roman

Catholicism in the 14th and 15th centuries. The popes of that time built a magnificent palace in Avignon and contributed greatly to its art and prosperity. Emily was particularly interested in the city because 12 years earlier she had taken an art course in Avignon. We located the old studio where she studied; it was still in operation.

We left our cruising companions in Avignon and moved on down the river. Soon, the mighty Alps were faintly visible in the distance to the east, newly crowned with glistening white snow. Farther down the river we were able to just make out the Pyrenees to the west. We passed ancient feudal towns and castles reminding us that this area was once more Roman than Rome, at least for a few centuries. A huge Roman coliseum, almost rivaling the one in Rome, was of interest to us in Arles.

We passed through the Côtes du Rhône wine country and took time to visit the Hermitage Cellars where we sent a few bottles of their best home to our relatives and friends. There we learned the meaning of the strange word langiappe (pronounced lan-yap) as we were offered one by the attendant. A langiappe is a small gift of some value given to one who has just made a purchase. We accepted a professional-style corkscrew and bottle opener.

Soon after Avignon, we entered the Petit Rhône, a much narrower river and probably a part of the Rhône delta, as we were now nearly at sea level. This led us off to the right and toward the Canal du Rhône a Sète. We soon entered it and were in a new environment—the Camargue, which is composed of swamplands dotted with many lakes called etangs. The area is supposed to be inhabited by wild white horses and pink flamingos. We were delighted to see both. A substantial flock of the beautiful birds flew low over us one afternoon and landed in a small etang up ahead. We saw many other flocks. We saw many of the white horses also, but since they were in pastures and barnyards they could not have been very wild. They were of the proper breed, however, and had probably been corralled and tamed. A few wild herds are still in the Parc de Camargue but we were not fortunate enough to see one.

We spent a couple of nights at a picturesque town called Aigues Mortes. It was a walled city with a huge refuge tower at one end. The walls were intact and in good shape. We strolled through the town and except for the clothes and the passage of an occasional auto, we realized it could have been lifted right out of the 13th century.

We were tempted to try to take a short canal out into the Mediterranean, but we were unable to get our masts raised and no one was willing to tell us that we could make it all the way with a 1.5 meter draft. We elected to press on to Sète for another reason—our visas were expiring in a few days and Emily was quite concerned about it.

We arrived in Sète early in the afternoon and I went immediately to the local police office. They did not seem the least concerned that our visas were expiring, and when I asked, "How long can we stay?" they answered, "How long do you need?" With that matter taken care of, we looked around for some way to get our masts stepped.

There were only two places that we had heard of, a large shipyard at the mouth of the harbor and a fishing-boating club in the center of the city. We visited the harbor and were disappointed in the moorage. We were told that it would be several days before they could get to us. While there, the fishing trawlers came in at top speed, let out their nets, and made several circles to wash them. This created lots of rocking and bouncing among the boats in the marina. It did not look like a great place to spend a single day let alone several. As a result, we investigated the club in town. A Swiss former tugboat captain whom we met near the club agreed to translate and discuss the operation. Arrangements were made and the next day we moved to the club's pier.

We waited for somebody to come, but nobody did. The next day our Swiss friend went into action and contacted someone who came down and looked at our boat.

"Impossible!" he said.

That is one French word that I have learned to understand (it is pronounced im-pos-eebl).

Our Swiss friend came over and saved our day by discussing the operation with the man who turned out to be the club chairman. The Swiss knew his business, having been the superintendent of a shipyard. The chairman changed from "C'est impossible" to "Peut être c'est possible" (perhaps it is possible).

As a result, the next day about 12 p.m. Frenchmen showed up and talked excitedly among themselves, pointing to the boat and gesticulating energetically. I could not find out who was in charge or what they were going to do. Soon they untied Golden Bell and moved it under the crane. It was then that I discovered that the crane was hand operated and swung freely. I began to feel nervous as the men swarmed on and off the boat talking in staccato French. I kept trying to tell them that it was my boat and that I would direct the operation. I was totally ignored and frequently shoved aside.

The Swiss gentlemen came over and assured me that I had nothing to fear. Hah! Easy for him to say. It wasn't his boat and he knew what they were saying. Finally, at his suggestion, I backed off and sort of closed my eyes and prayed. I'd like to say that when I opened them the masts were up. It was not that way. They struggled and cursed (I'm sure) and finally a half-hour later the two masts were in place. Actually, considering that the crane was not quite high enough, they did a marvelous job. We had tea in the clubhouse later and they made us honorary members.

Now, with the masts up, we were ready to go to sea. There was only one small problem—one more bridge to negotiate in order to gain access to the sea. We had already passed through four bridges which were open only twice a day at precise times. We dutifully telephoned the bridge and arranged for its opening at 9:00 a.m. We were circling in front of it at the appointed time but nothing happened. We kept circling for an hour and still nothing happened.

Tired of going in circles, we moored near the bridge office and saw that there were men present. We couldn't understand why they didn't open the bridge. Emily went ashore and climbed the stairs to the bridge office where she spent 10 or 15 minutes. She returned to the boat, with a wry smile, and said, "It's another greve" (a strike).

"When will it be over?" I asked.

"They don't know, it all depends on talks in Paris. They were told to go on strike, so they did," Emily replied.

By now we had developed into much better Frenchmen, so we secured our mooring lines there in the middle of town next to the bus stop and settled down patiently to wait.

Emily made a couple more trips up to the office to check on developments. The men seemed to enjoy her visits though they could tell her nothing. Along about 5:00 p.m. the next day, we heard the clanging of the bridge barricades and so I prepared to cast off.

"Shouldn't we check with the bridge tenders to make sure that we can get through?" asked Emily.

"Absolutely not. If that bridge opens, we are going through, I promise you," I said. It did and we did! We now had access to the sea. We were awed by several freighters coming in from their anchorage off the shore. We learned later that the bridges were opened to let them in, but none could go out, except us, of course. As we passed the opened bridge there were three Frenchmen standing on the pier one resplendent with a tricolor sash. One of them shouted, "Have a nice treep." They were glad that we were able to continue—the French are nice people, just patsies for labor leaders.

We were now a couple of harbors away from the Golfe du Lion hoping to harbor hop to Barcelona from where we were. Our intermediate objective was to get past the dreaded Cap de Creus which sort of terminates the Pyrenees and defines the Golfe. With good weather we would be in Barcelona in one week. With the kind of weather we had been getting it would probably take three weeks. I've learned a new French word tempete—meaning gale. I hope we don't run into one.

We will write again from Barcelona. Till then, fair winds and snug harbors.

Love,
Paul and Emily

SITGES, SPAIN

11

Sitges,
Spain
May 2, 1987

Dear Friends,

This little town of Sitges is just south of Barcelona. It is a fascinating and historic town with ancient cathedrals and topless beaches vying for our attention. We are now finished with the upgrading of Golden Bell, which we accomplished in a shipyard in Barcelona and this winter's experience left us with many memories of this beautiful, romantic city.

One of our strongest memories was our visit to the

Picasso Museum where we spent four hours. Emily, who has an inexhaustible appetite for art in any form, finally said, "I've had enough for one day." Barcelona has produced some remarkable artists who were different. In addition to Picasso, Dali (although Dali was not of this area) painted here a lot and, of course, spawned a whole new school of surrealism. Picasso's museum was, well, interesting.

We spent an entire day on Gaudi, a most remarkable architect. He has several buildings and a garden here in Barcelona and designed light fixtures and benches in wrought iron for the major boulevard. His greatest work is the Familia Segrada, a cathedral that is abuilding. It will probably not be finished for another 50 to 75 years. How to describe his designs—rather like a taste for martinis; it has to be acquired, and once acquired is intoxicating. We grew to like it very much and wonder why more buildings are not built like this, with curves and designs that tickle the fancy. (Answer: it is too expensive for investors to take seriously when they can build boxes more cheaply.)

The many other galleries and gardens devoted to art make Barcelona not only beautiful, but certainly one of the art capitals of the world.

A second memory might be called "The Thieves of Barcelona." We think we have met most of them. While you may decry their objectives, you have to admire their skill and professionalism.

Item one: Our first day in Barcelona, a beautiful summer day, crowds strolling along the street, I felt a tap on my shoulder and a smiling young man was pointing to my back. Reaching around I felt something gooey and sticky. The young man also pointed to Emily's back containing some globs of white stuff. The young man whipped out a large tissue and offered it to us, and clucking sounds of condolence directed us to a bench where we could wipe it off. Such a nice young man! Just then I arrived at the bench and moved Emily's purse out of the way to put down my jacket. At that point an older English couple walked up and cautioned Emily, "Don't put down your purse or they will grab it." The young man started to edge away as I picked up the purse and turned to look at him. Just then the gentleman yelled several times, "Guardia! Guardia!" The nice young man fled at top speed stripping off a back pack he was carrying. The gentleman explained that this was a standard ploy by the thieves. They have a spray can of white stuff that I suppose they purchase at the supermarket for thieves, brigands, and cutpurses. In a dense crowd they spray you with it and you are unaware of it. They offer to help and to focus your attention onto the glob and away from purse or wallet.

Incident two remains a mystery. We lost both our cameras, a small ghetto blaster, and a bunch of lenses. We think that someone came aboard Golden Bell while we were asleep (scary!). Another possibility is that we could have left a hatch unlocked when we went to the store. We think the former is correct because a cat burgler was known to be operating in the area. We had to admire his skill also.

Incident three was exciting and had a happy ending. I was having lunch at one of my favorite restaurants on the Plaza de Catalunya. It's called MacDonalds and my favorite meal there, a sandwich called a Beeg Mak, strips of potato fried in deep fat called Tatos, and a cerveza (beer). I set my bright red backpack down next to my feet and opened my copy of the International Herald Tribune prepared to enjoy this exotic Spanish cuisine.

Out of the corner of my eye I saw a red blob rise and move away from my feet. Jumping up I saw my backpack sailing over the heads of some people and being caught by a man at the door. I saw red again, but this time it was generated from within my eyes. I knew I would never catch the man at the door, but his partner was still in reach, his progress stopped by a group of people going up the short flight of stairs to the door. I grabbed him by the shoulders and threw him to the floor. I probably would never see my pack again but, by gum, this man was going to jail!

As I started to straddle his back I saw another red blob settle down on the stairs. My pack had mysteriously appeared on the steps! I had my pack back and realized the futility of bringing charges against him—so I picked up my pack and returned to my meal. The MacDonalds people rushed over asking, "Que Pasa?" The man I had intercepted at the door, far from being angry for my treating him so roughly, loudly proclaimed his innocence and edged for the door.

When you think about it, it was very clever what they did—they just lost this one because of a stubborn American who doesn't like to be pushed around. The principal snatches the purse or bag or whatever and tosses it quickly to a confederate near the door who waits just long enough to make sure that everything is all right with his partner. The partner, who has nothing in his hand, protests his innocence and is sure that you are mistaken. They rendezvous later. But every once in a while some darned fool American gets mad and takes physical action instead of just talking and yelling. In this case the article was deposited on the floor in sight of the crazy man. "Now what had been stolen, Senor?"

A fourth technique was demonstrated to some friends of ours from New Zealand who are living on their boat here in Sitges. In spite of our cautions, the wife set her purse down at the side of a bench as they sat—after all there was a thick hedge in back of it. A very pleasant Spanish gentleman speaking rather good English engaged them in conversation. Suddenly his facial expression changed and he walked away and there was a commotion behind the couple.

A Guardia handed the lady her purse that he had just taken from a man on the other side of the hedge. They walked the man over to a wall, spread-eagled him and worked over his kidneys a little with their nightsticks. This was Spanish justice; you are caught in the act, you get punished—now! The thief probably never went to jail, but I suspect his days in Barcelona are numbered. I give you these details for your protection in case you decide to attend the Summer Olympics in Barcelona in 1992.

Speaking of the Olympics, already streets were being widened, overpasses constructed and ground cleared for the stadium and buildings. This happened not far from where we were moored in Barcelona. This will make a beautiful city even more beautiful. Barcelona's streets are dominated by many tree-lined boulevards with many beautiful buildings. There are many Gaudiesque buildings and none over five or six stories high.

The Rambla is Barcelona's most exciting street. You start at the Plaza de Catalunya in the center of the shopping district with its many fountains and statues. You must first elbow your way through a few gatherings of political debaters and then you begin to stroll between flower shops and bird stalls. The riot of color is almost overwhelming, the singing of the canaries soothes the ear. The center of the street is the Rambla (walk) and just a single auto lane exists on either side to provide some commercial access to the fine shops that line the sides. If you continue long enough, you arrive at the impressive statue of Christopher Columbus on the harbor drive. He stands there, high on a column, surrounded by adulating statues and fountains, and points to the west.

The entire city is served by similar boulevards of lesser beauty, but lined with handsome buildings, shaded by trees carefully pruned, and often with a promenade in the center. Fountains, statues, and flowers are usually in the many small squares or plazas (courts) that occur when two streets come together or terminate.

Most buildings have wrought iron balconies and in the less opulent areas they are decorated with the family's daily wash. It is virtually impossible to walk in any residential area without hearing the songs of the canaries. Most households seem to have them and they set them out on the balcony in the sunshine during the day. These happy little creatures then fill the air with their songs.

The old town area was not far from our moorage so we visited it often. The narrow streets are charming but a little hazardous. Autos are forbidden but what is so interesting is that youngsters on motor-scooters, and oldsters for that matter, go roaring through the narrow streets, grazing pedestrians and ignoring intersections as though they were alone in the world. The area contains many of the art museums and galleries, smart shops, and of course, many sidewalk cafes.

Our saga of Barcelona would not be complete without mention of Mamoon. Mamoon was a squatter who lived in the scrapyard of the boatyard where we spent the winter. He lived in a big piece of pipe, had two vinyl-covered easy chairs, and a couple of pots and pans. Occasionally he went out with the sardine fleet, but mostly he just drank wine. He ran the small camp there and other down-and-outers (including a woman) came and went but Mamoon was always there. We gave him money and food from time to time and he agreed to watch our boat. He even recovered a Polaroid camera for us that he said a boy had picked up from our boat deck.

When I told a port security officer that I thought Mamoon might have taken the things off our boat in our absence, he strongly insisted that this could not happen. You see, the code is to strongly defend your territory from any suspicion. Mamoon might have gone to some other area to pick up a few things, but never, absolutely never! would he allow theft to occur in his own territory.

Most of our time in Barcelona was spent in the shipyard getting work done on the boat. Three impressions remain of that chapter of our life: the sardine fleet, the dirty harbor, and the proud skill of the workmen.

I wanted a certain thing done on the boat and communicated this to the carpenter. The carpenter refused and wanted to do it his way. After several minutes of arguing, during which neither of us understood the other, he walked off the boat. I went to the shipyard manager, who spoke good English, and asked him to explain to Juan that I had my reasons and besides it was my boat and he must do it my way.

A half-hour later the carpenter returned and somewhat meekly said, "Comprendo, es su barco" (I understand, it is your boat). I have to admit that he was an artist in wood and the results were beautiful. However, if you want something done a certain way you must supervise these artisans as they will ignore drawings and instructions in the interest of turning out fine work.

And now for the sardine fleet! We were moored just across the harbor from the fleet at the Taleres Pons shipyard. Each morning very early, the fleet left and returned about mid-day with its catch. The sardine boats are about 40-50 feet long and one side is stacked with empty crates about the size of a peach crate. Each drags an auxiliary boat with it and on the stern of the auxiliary are two large metal dishes pointing at the water. These are floodlights. The tender is cut loose and turns on the flood and the sardines are attracted to the light. The mother boat circles the tender with the net and closes it. The men haul it up and scoop the sardines into the crates. Then they race back to the quay, just across from us, where they sell their catch. The first few in get the best price. As they come in, the tender is cut loose and a man in it with oars awaits the return of the mother ship from the loading dock which then ties up until the next morning. The men are paid off with a few pesetas and a bag of sardines. As I mentioned, Mamoon would go out with them occasionally and he always offered us some sardines. Emily accepted some once and tried pickling them. I suppose that they are a delicacy to many.

For the final anecdote let me tell you of a very nice thing that happened to us. We had just come into Spain after two days spent pinned down by the wind in a deserted port just behind Cap de Creus. After this delay, we were hurrying south toward Barcelona. We made an intermediate stop at the small port of Blanes. As we tied up at the visitor's quay, a man with a proper British accent walked up and introduced himself, "I am Gunter Reich. Welcome to Blanes."

"That sounds quite German," I said.

"There's a good reason for that. I am German from Frankfurt. I learned my English in school from an Englishman and although I spent four years in America, I never lost the British accent." Gunter had been trying to reach us on a hand-held marine radio from his villa high on a cliff just north of Blanes. Since we didn't respond on the radio, when he saw us turn into the port of Blanes, he decided to come down and welcome us. "I imagine you would enjoy a shower, so come on up to my house and bring your toothbrush so you can spend the night."

To a couple who had just had a long bout with the sea, this sounded like angels singing. We accepted. We stopped at a supermarket where he purchased a rabbit and began to talk glowingly of the dinner he was planning for us tomorrow.

Soon we were sitting on his veranda, which was just above his swimming pool, high on a cliff over the blue Mediterranean. During the next few days, six to be exact, he exploited his considerable skill as a gourmet cook. We went through spareribs, squab, chicken, rabbit, and a marvelous bouillabaisse. These we topped off with excellent wines, brandies, and liqueurs.

Gunter, as is the habit of many Europeans, planned his big meal for the mid-day, and at night he had only a glass of wine and a lard (yes, I said lard) sandwich. He was single, retired, and divided his time between Germany, where his son looked after his house and motor cruiser, and his villa on the Costa Brava. He was well read and quite ready to talk on any subject and perhaps knew more about American politics and issues than I did. We do read newspapers and magazines when we can find English editions. *Time, Newsweek, Penthouse, and Playboy* magazines are found on foreign newsstands as are *The International Herald Tribune* and *USA Today* newspapers. But I digress—Emily, Gunter, and I had many fine conversations by the fire in the evening over a glass of sherry.

    The town of Sitges is just south of Barcelona, and we quit that noisy, dirty harbor as soon as the repairs on the boat were completed.

    We are looking forward to a visit from our son, Tom, and his wife, Becky, in another week. We will take the train into Barcelona to share the delights of that city with them, and then sail to the Balearics, a group of islands about 100 miles off the coast of Spain in the Mediterranean.

    After Tom and Becky leave, it is our plan to return to the U.S. and Oregon where we plan to upgrade our ham licenses, attend my 50th class reunion (you didn't think I was that old, did you? Well, did you?), and take care of a lot of business. Of course, we will visit with relatives and friends. One of Emily's longings has been to fly the Concorde, the supersonic plane to France and England. We will do that one way. We arrive in New York a couple of hours before we leave London. I'll try not to be so long before the next letter.

In the mean time, keep well and happy.

Love,
    Paul and Emily

12

Island of Mikonos,
Greece
August 31, 1987

Dear Friends,

  In the *Rogues Guide to Corfu,* David Louison says that when an Italian runs afoul of the law, he goes to Sicily and hides in the hills. When an American is in trouble, he goes to Chicago where another gangster, more or less, is not noticed. When a Greek has this fugitive, problem he goes to Corfu and assumes the name of Spiro. It is estimated that two-thirds of the male population of the island is named Spiro after the patron saint of Corfu, Saint

Spirodon. The saint's presence is strongly felt everywhere and his corporeal remains are carefully preserved, some say miraculously, in the principal cathedral of the city.

I viewed the remains myself by standing in line behind an old woman in widow's garb. When her turn came to approach the sepulcher, after some discussion with the two priests guarding it, she kissed the sandled foot which was exposed, a brass plaque in the center, and the glass that covered the exposed, severed head. She was, I presume, asking the good saint for a special miracle for herself—for this is the saint's business.

Saint Spirodon has been credited with innumerable miracles since his first, about 320 AD. He has been given credit for stopping invasions, winning wars, curing body lice, and, rather artfully, I think, curing a plague by changing it into a pussycat and sending it to Naples. He is very busy with miracles, as you can see, but still finds time to be the patron saint of ships at sea. That was the purpose of my visit, to seek his blessing on our future voyages.

Needless to say, we found Corfu totally charming, with its Citadel, its narrow streets, its hundreds of tables under the trees in the squares, the daily, sometimes hourly, band concerts, and the many horse-drawn carriages. It was easy to understand why it is a favorite haunt of vacationing Englishmen and backpacking European youth. Corfu also boasted indifferent trash pickup and the smelliest harbor we had yet encountered.

You may recall that we left Golden Bell in Mallorca, one of the Balaeric Islands off the coast of Spain, while we went home to the U. S. for a visit. Returning, we provisioned Golden Bell and set off for the next island in the group, Menorca. Menorca is a different cruising experience. Its shore-line consists of many calas, which are holes in a rocky cliff with a harbor inside and a small beach at the head. Usually there is room for only a few boats to anchor inside but the ones already in will offer to take a line ashore or suggest you raft with them. There is also access from the land and the tourists enjoy these small, intimate beaches.

At one of the calas where we stopped, there were numerous caves of ancient origin that were still occupied. The natives were mainly distinguished by the fact that they wore no clothes. The yachties and sun worshippers who visited this beach, out of respect for the natives, I suppose, undressed similarly. We watched them; they watched us.

The major harbor on Menorca is Mahon. It is a large, well-protected bay and is easily defended. The nation that controlled it controlled the western Mediterranean. As a consequence, it has changed hands many times in its history, depending on the force supreme of the moment. When it was in French hands, Cardinal Richelieu had a special sauce served at a banquet celebrating France's occupation of the island. Although the sauce was served in Paris, it was invented by the cardinal's chef and named Mahon-aise. It is a staple in most homes today.

The day before we left, we observed a ceremony enacted by the local fishermen and common to all Catholic maritime provinces. The local priest is taken out in a fishing boat to the entrance to the harbor where a wreath is tossed onto the water and a blessing spoken. It is a day for all the boats in a community. They are gaily decorated and follow the wake of the priest in a watery procession. Celebrations usually occur in the late afternoon and when night falls, huge bonfires are lit on the beaches around the harbor. Any boat is welcome to participate. We declined, but some of the cruisers in the harbor did join the fleet with all flags flying.

From Menorca we took off on an overnight to the Italian island of Sardinia. Before leaving, we had met a young couple, Ray and Debbie, on the boat named Only Child. They were heading in the same direction and, because we were seasoned passage-makers, they asked if they might accompany us. We accepted and their presence was comforting and pleasant. During the night, their lights were a beacon and each two hours at the change of watch we checked in with them on the radio, comparing positions and making sure everything was going well. We both had Loran—a radio location device that used several stations operated by the military. Under certain conditions our location could be fixed to within a few feet.

Golden Bell was as fast as their light displacement boat when going with the wind and I was very proud of her speed. When the wind turned forward of the beam, however, Only Child soon was a speck on the horizon. The saying is, "When you have two sailors on the same ocean, you have a race." I trimmed and fussed and fumed but still trailed.

When we arrived at Sardinia, it was late at night, so we elected to heave-to for the rest of the night rather than try to enter a strange harbor in the dark. In addition to many other good traits, Ray and Debbie had a fondness for popcorn. During the next few days when we traveled together, our evenings were spent with a glass of wine and a bowl of popcorn and much pleasant conversation.

From Sardinia we had another overnight to the

island of Ustica, a small island of the Aeolian group. We also visited Limparo and Vulcano. The later is mostly a heap of volcanic ash of recent origin and a still-bubbling crater.

Anchoring on Vulcano was a bit chancy so I stayed onboard while Emily, Ray, and Debbie climbed the crater to view the bubble and smell the smoke. Bored with my solitude and the hot day, I took a short nap after lunch. When I awoke, I was about a mile out to sea. The anchor had dragged into deep water. I finally motored sheepishly up to the dock where the shore party awaited me.

"We knew you had taken a nap and hoped that you wouldn't drift into trouble. We could see you from the crater." And that was all those nice people said.

From Vulcano, we made a short hop to Sicily and the next day transited the Straits of Messina. These, you may recall, are the perilous straits through which Ulysses passed safely by stuffing cotton in the ears of his crew and by having himself tied to the mast. The Songs of the Sirens were supposed to lure the boats onto the rocks of Scilla. He, of course, made it safely through the gnashing rocks in spite of his mad ravings to the crew, which ignored him.

In the August, 1986 issue of *National Geographic*, Tim Severin makes a strong, almost undisputable, case for the placement of Scilla and Charybdis at the north end of the island of Levkas instead of between the island of Sicily and mainland Italy. That location makes much more sense than the traditional one which would have required that Ulysses make a detour of some 250 miles from his course home to Ithaca. Highly improbable in the small, open boats of those days.

When Emily and I transited the straits, she

threatened to tie me to the mast, but didn't. It turned out all right as the Sirens were apparently out to lunch.

Not far on the other side of the straits was the small harbor of Reggio de Calabra on the mainland. From here, hydrofoils sped across to Sicily and other islands in the vicinity. These interesting boats lower a small hydrodynamic blade in the water and with a powerful motor make the transit with only the propeller and the blade in the water. Speeds of 30 to 60 miles per hour are common and they can carry from 30 to 100 passengers or more. In Regio we parted company with Only Child as Ray and Debbie were going to Sicily where they planned to leave their boat while they returned to the States for a year or two. We were pressing on to Greece and hoped to winter in Turkey.

One afternoon a young, blond American woman approached us and said, "The marina manager says that you-all are going to Greece." (Question: How come we run into so many Texans over here?) We allowed as to how we were.

"My name is Debbie," she said, "and I'm knocking around the Med and would like to go to Greece. And eventually to Turkey. I could take the train, but I think it would be fun to go on a boat. I can cook, stand watch, clean, and do whatever you want and will pay a little bit," she said.

We conversed for a while and then welcomed her aboard. Let me explain why we were glad that she had been available. We think that two hours is about as long as anyone can stay alert on watch, especially during the night. When we make a long passage with just us two onboard, that means two-hour watches for each of us on a 24-hour basis. They interrupt our biorhythms and it takes several days to adjust. During that time we are chronically fatigued.

When a third person is available to stand watch, that means two hours on and four hours off, enabling each person to have two deep-sleep periods during the night.

As it was, Debbie proved to be a delightful asset for the boat. She spoke Italian rather well, was eager to assist in the ship's routine, and learned quickly. She awakened for watches cheerfully (well, almost) and didn't get seasick (well, not quite). She had been backpacking around Europe for more than a year on a Eurail Pass, as are thousands of other youths from other countries. She thought crewing on a yacht would be a new experience. She had her experience and we got our rest.

Two nights and three days after leaving Reggio, we entered a delightful small bay and harbor on Paxos, a small island just south of Corfu. The next day, we motored through the calm to the island and city of Corfu. After checking in through Greek customs, we sorrowfully bid good-bye to Debbie as she boarded a bus for Istanbul.

Incidentally, for the benefit of the cruisers and cruisers-to-be who read this, what we did was not a good idea. We should have been much more cautious about signing on a crewperson, especially in foreign countries. We knew little about Debbie. She could have had drugs stashed in her pack and could have been a fugitive, or worse she could have made all kinds of accusations for which our boat could have been impounded and the skipper, me, tossed into jail. We have done this twice and lucked out both times with fine young people. But, more caution should have been exercised.

We love Greece so far and especially Corfu. Almost everybody speaks some English and the people are naturally outgoing and friendly. One day on a walk in the outskirts of the city, Emily and I paused and gazed admiringly through an archway into a charming courtyard. At one end was a medallion carved of stone.

A man standing there noticed our interest and said, "The medallion is over 1,000 years old." He then inquired, "Where are you from?"

When we said "America," he laughingly said, "Not Dallas, I hope."

We quickly and vehemently denied that affiliation and groaned sympathetically with his relief to find that we were not rich, hard-driving, selfish, adulterous Texans. With that he introduced himself as Napoleon and his friend as Marie. We talked awhile longer and then Marie excused herself. We called after her, "You have a very nice day now, Marie." She paused, turned, fumbled in her shopping bag and took out a small white flower which she handed to Emily.

Our ultimate destination for this fall was Athens and the Cyclades, islands of myths and ancient heroes. We left Corfu in somewhat of a hurry to make connections in Athens with a friend, Kathy Woodson, who was planning to join us there in one week. Our schedule called for 24 to 30 miles per day. There was little or no wind so we foresaw no problem motoring that far each day.

We took a half-day off and visited the site of Delphi. At one time, about 3,000 years ago, give or take 500 years, this was considered the center of the universe. In fact, we have a picture of the stone that marked the exact center of the universe, according to the scholars of that time.

This was also the site of the Oracle of Delphi. She guided the destiny of so many great men of that time. Many of the Ceasars, the great heroes, and kings of this era, journeyed to this spot to consult the oracle before launching a military or political campaign. We saw the rock where the oracle sat suspended in a chair held up by three poles. The oracle was a temple maiden who was in touch with Apollo (some say through drugs) and who gave very vague and generalized predictions.

The site of Delphi is high on the steep slope of a mountain. The view is breathtaking. Below, a couple of thousand feet, is a sea of olive trees that stretches to the blue Mediterranean in the distance. When one travels as much as we do, one becomes a little calloused about new experiences, but Delphi was unforgettable, humbling, and completely unique.

As you turn from drinking in the valley panorama, you see a zigzag pathway climbing the slope above you. As you climb this path you pass old ruins, some partially restored. To approach the temple of Apollo, you must pass these buildings called treasuries. There you place the gift that you have brought to your god. Some of the finest art treasures of this time have been recovered here, including the magnificent bronze stature of the Charioteer and probably the finest statue of Zeus ever found. These I recall from my ancient history studies in grammar school.

An earthquake apparently toppled most everything, but much restoration has taken place and the effort continues. Restored was an almost complete amphitheater that used to entertain the mighty and the wealthy, and a sports stadium which contained about the only level ground of any size in the area. As we stood there in the entrance arches of the stadium you could almost hear the cheering of the spectators as they urged on their favorite warrior (or, perhaps, the lion).

Another somewhat awesome experience was our transit of the Corinth Canal. The Peloponnesian peninsula is separated from the Greek mainland by a rather narrow (about 6.5 kilometers, or four miles) land bridge, which, according to the bad news, is solid rock. The good news is that the rock is limestone, which is a soft rock. Corinth, was a major seaport on the west side of this peninsula and Corinthian sailors were well known for their skill in plying the Mediterranean. To the east lay the great spice and silk sources, and of course, Jerusalem, the center of Christianity. St. Paul wrote a couple of letters to the small colony of Christians living in Corinth.

The alternative to unloading ships and transporting by camel across the narrow peninsula was to take a long and somewhat perilous detour around the south end of the peninsula. Even in the time of Jesus, there was talk of the need of a canal, and excavation was actually begun in 67 AD. The canal was not seriously pursued until 1881 and was completed in 1893.

To travel this canal, you approach either end and await the raising of a blue flag. Traffic is only allowed to move in one direction at a time and when we arrived at Corinth the red flag was up. We circled just outside the rather small harbor, although 1800 years ago it probably was a big one, and two motorboats passed us and went on in, but of course, they had to wait also. Soon a small flotilla of motorboats emerged from the canal and the blue flag went up.

Ahead of us there appeared a small split in the hill. From the harbor it looked hardly wide enough for passage, but if the powerboats could chance it, so could we! There was a current in the canal and Golden Bell, with its small diesel auxiliary motor, could make good only about three miles per hour.

We were now between sheer rock walls that rose several hundred feet above us. In two places there were bridges flung across this man-made gorge for the motor traffic to cross. We had lunch under way, and were thoroughly enjoying ourselves when we approached the end. The two motor vessels had long since vanished ahead of us. Now, we saw where the bridge was open at the opposite end, a man gesticulating wildly in an angry manner—"Hurry up! Hurry up!" he was clearly saying. We had our motor wide open so there was nothing we could do. As we passed through the small bridge opening, he shouted something which I'm glad I couldn't understand. So I just shrugged my shoulders with my hands held open to him in a supplicating manner and slowly continued on.

On the other side, we pulled up to the quay, as ordered, and paid our fee of about $170, which made this the most expensive four miles we have ever traveled by any means of transportation. Another American yacht was tied up near us so we walked over to chat a bit. They were quitting the blankety-blank Aegean Sea as the meltemi was spoiling everything. They were going to the other side of Greece for some enjoyable cruising, by golly! We had heard of this meltemi before, but after all, we were world cruisers and an occasional strong wind is a part of the cruising life right?

The meltemi is a strong wind that blows out of the

northeast and sweeps across the Aegean Sea, through the Greek islands of the Cyclades, and out into the open sea where it loses its energy. It starts about the first of July and is usually over by mid-September. You will have two to three days of twenty to thirty-knot winds and two to three days of mild winds or none at all.

Undeterred, we pressed on and rendezvoused with Kathy in Athens. On our first day out of Athens—which we failed to visit—we experienced the meltemi. From no wind in the morning, a breeze sprang up and grew stronger as the day waxed. We were moving east along the southern shore of the Athenian peninsula and were somewhat protected from the wind. Our destination was an island just off the nose of the peninsula. The seas became rougher and rougher so we elected not to go to the island, but to head upwind a few miles and drop anchor in a protected bay on the peninsula. We could not make any progress under sail against the wind so we turned on the motor and tried to motor into it. The strong wave force and the pressure on the spars and rigging of the boat held us at a virtual standstill.

By quartering the seas and exhibiting absolute glee at our progress of one-half mile per hour, we eventually (two hours later) nosed into the bay and relatively calm water.

There was a small village at the head of the bay, so when the anchor was down and the evening wind had subsided a little, we unshipped the dinghy and went ashore. At the small restaurant, we had some difficulty with the menu; it was Greek to us and the proprietor had difficulty with our English. Finally, he beckoned to us and we followed him out to the kitchen. From the savory pots of food and other viands awaiting our pleasure, we selected a most satisfying meal.

These people were among the friendliest, most cheerful of any we have met on our travels. Proving, I suppose, that language is only a mild deterrent to friendship among people. We washed down our meal with a bottle of fine Greek wine as we sat there at an outdoor table and watched the sun set behind the low hills. A dinghy ride back to Golden Bell, whose anchor light sparkled in the moonless night, capped a day that had begun good, turned bad, then turned good again. Such is the life of a world cruiser.

As I write we are pinned down by a furious gale in the harbor of Mikonos, one of the major tourist islands of the Cyclades. The last time we were in winds this strong was in the South Pacific. This time, fortunately, we are tied to a stone quay, and although the wind shrieks in the rigging, the water is relatively smooth here in the harbor.

We had left the next day for Mikonos in relatively calm morning weather, hoping that the meltemi would not show up to smite us. Wrong! About 10:00 a.m. we got a nice breeze so we hoisted the sails. For a while, all was well. Then the wind got a little strong and we were out from under the peninsula's shelter so the waves kicked up a bit. By noon we had reefed (reduced) sail. By 2:00 p.m. we were under a stabilizing sail and had the motor going, approaching Mikonos. The waves were high and we were rolling with gusto.

Finally, about 3:00 p.m. we sighted the harbor—and a bunch of nasty rocks in front of it in an ideal position so that if the motor failed, we would be set down upon them. We came in on a reefed main and a prayer that the motor would not fail us. Soon we could see the smooth water inside the harbor at about 400 meters. This slowly reduced as we made our way and our troubles were over! We were soon tied to the stone quay. That was three days ago and the meltemi has not yet let up. In fact, it has grown stronger. The local fishermen do not know when it will stop, so it looks like Kathy is going to spend a lot more time in Mikonos than she had planned. We are used to this sort of thing but she has a two-week limit to her vacation.

Perhaps the couple heading west through the Corinth Canal had it right. In the meantime, keep well and happy.

Love,
Paul and Emily

13

Kusadasi,
Turkey
November 19, 1987

Dear Friends,

  These last few months have been a mixed but exciting blend of wonderful experiences and frustrating experiences. But then, that is the way of the cruising life. We do not spend all of our time sailing on smooth seas in gentle breezes to snug harbors in exotic places where curious but pleasant people live in a quaint style. Sometimes the seas are stormy, the harbors are dirty, the people are uncommunicative or hostile, the harbors are crowded and ringed with high-rise condos, the officials are difficult, the prices are staggering, and your anchor drags in the night. Furthermore, you can't find any of the amenities, such as peanut butter or brown sugar, to which you have been accustomed. Sometimes your prop gets fouled, you lose your favorite knife overboard while diving in a filthy harbor to cut your prop free while a ferry loaded with people waits for you to get the— out of their mooring space. Why do we do it? Because we love it!

The farther east we went in the Mediterranean, the more primitive things became. We smarted under the telephone system in France, but it was modern and efficient compared to those in Turkey and Greece. Shops for almost anything became smaller and the chances were if you were looking for something special you might have to visit several stores before you found it—if you ever did. Supermarkets and the concept of one-stop shopping had not penetrated into any but the largest of cities. We, of course, spent most of our time in the small coastal towns; the harbors of the larger towns were abhorrent examples of crowded, dirty, noisy, smelly environments. The marinas that existed might be near the large cities but they were seldom in the main harbor. If they were, they were usually occupied by fishing boats.

Instead of harboring in these, we anchored in bays where we were the only, or nearly the only, boat and dinghyed ashore to clean beaches or village quays. We have anchored within a few meters of ancient fortifications and other assorted ruins, wandered through streets too narrow or too vertical to support vehicle traffic and where the only transportation was donkeys, visited abbeys built into the face of a nearly vertical cliff, and dropped anchor in a remote bay where the call of the muezzin floated over the water from the small mosque while cows trudged solemnly along the beach toward their evening milking. We have snorkeled over schools of fish so numerous and so brightly colored as to dazzle the eyes, and along vertical cliffs that soared hundreds of feet over our heads and dropped an equal amount into the abysmal depths containing caves and crevices that we had not the courage to explore. We have lazed on sunny beaches where we learned that if you see two you haven't seen them all. We have shared a glass of ouzo and a piece of rosewater candy in the above abbey with a quiet monk and marveled at the drive that compels men to build in such a place where the construction difficulties were all but insurmountable and isolation was complete. We have wandered through outdoor markets covering several acres and containing the most beautiful vegetables and fruits that we had ever seen, and through streets lined with the merchants of rugs, brass and leather. And finally, on a chilly evening, we sat in the cocoon of our floating home in that foreign land of friendly people, snugged down for the winter. Here we have half-formed plans to see more of this historic and fascinating country, and perhaps a little more of Europe, and to get a few things done on the boat.

  Winter here, in this part of Turkey, means frequent storms varying in intensity, and rain, but no snow or ice. When the sun shines and the wind doesn't blow, it seems almost tropical. Confirmation of this climate was in the form of large fields of cotton. Each day the sun sinks a little closer to the southern horizon to remind us that winter approaches and that it will be a long time before we can again lie on the beaches and swim in the water. The latitude here is 38 degrees, about that of San Francisco.

The cruising community at Turban Kusadasi Marina is a fascinating blend of many nations. There are Germans, Italians, French, Brits (British), Canadians and Australians. Some, like us, planned to spend the winter, but many went home for the holiday season or longer. We were a bit late coming in and many had already hauled out their boats and left for their homes, not to return until April or May. But a nice group of friendly people remained.

Perhaps you would like to know where we have been since our last letter from the Greek island of Mikonos in the Cyclades. We enjoyed the five days we were pinned down there in the harbor of Mikonos. The village was quite touristy, but still was interesting and contained all the features that a quaint Greek island village should have. The narrow streets wound between whitewashed one- and two-story buildings. There were cafes on the plazas here and there but the concentration seemed to be near the waterfront. A huge pelican wandered freely among the tables along the harbor, but he did make a pest of himself and the proprietors and waiters had to chase him out occasionally. The street vegetable and fish vendors were here and there, carefully weighing their customers' desires out on scales that resembled those of the Statue of Liberty.

Tired old stone windmills were perched on the hill in back of the town, but were no longer adorned with their huge blades. Little donkeys with their pack baskets were tethered here and there and were still used for transportation in the interior of the village, as an automobile or truck would have been unable to negotiate the narrow, winding streets. They were conveniently equipped with a pouch dangling under their tail. Widows dressed in black strolled about on their errands and sometimes stopped to talk to the bearded Orthodox priests sunning themselves on the benches. (In Greece, when a husband dies, his widow dons the widow's garb for the rest of her life or until she remarries. This is all black and includes a hood that covers the hair.)

Tied next to us on the quay was a Greek yacht that had been chartered by four American men and had a Greek skipper. Ordinarily this would have been of no great significance, but the Greek skipper was, according to the women on our boat and the three women on the boat next to ours, absolutely b-e-a-u-t-i-f-u-l! I just thought he was a nice guy. Also, one of the American men made a strong pitch for Kathy (remember, she joined us in Athens) who is a spectacular blond. This included a meal out for all four of us at the finest restaurant in the village and the pursuit continued for months after they returned to the U.S.

A slightly sour note was that we were showered with sand for several days as the meltemi continued and a barge was being loaded with sand nearby. The most offensive intrusion was a disco just across the street from us. They did not open until the other places closed at 1:00 a.m. and continued until 7:00 a.m.! I have no objection to people having fun in their own way but only if they do not invade others' rights and privacy!

We finally accepted the fact that this meltemi was not going to blow itself out in the near future, so we abandoned any plans to go to the islands north of us. And since going downwind was not too trying, we set out next for Paros during a slight lull in the storm. Paros was south and a little west of Mikonos and we had a wonderful sail downwind—until the wind died completely. This is what they say about sailing in the Mediterranean—you either have too much wind or none at all. We motored into Paros and moored to the town quay.

Kathy, after experiencing a couple of days on Paros, was anxious to get on to San Torini, a particularly spectacular island at the southern tip of the Cyclades. We, too, would have liked to have seen it, but we were expecting more friends from the States, and with the meltemi controlling our actions we would have had no other place to take our friends. Kathy took the ferry to San Torini and then back to Athens and home. Incidentally, if you want to see the Greek islands in a touring sense, our advice is: fly to Athens and then take the ferry to the islands. They run frequently and ignore the meltemi (almost—they were stormbound in Mikonos one day when the winds reached gale proportions). They are inexpensive and dependable, but unfortunately, not as clean as one would like.

Neil and Sonia Buist and Nancy Keneway joined us in Paros. They were less concerned with touring and more with experiencing. We rented absurd cars, such as Jeeps and dune buggies and visited a different ruin each day or a remote mountain village or abbey. We met quintessential Greeks in their own environments. We dallied in small tavernas and sunned and swam on clean, remote beaches. We then went on to Naxos and repeated this format. Neil and Sonia left us there but Nancy stayed on for a few more days and sailed with us to Skhinoussa. We had a light breeze all the way but dropped anchor about mid-afternoon in a small bay, well protected from the meltemi. We had three wonderful experiences on this remote and little-visited island. In the late afternoon, a local shepherd brought his flock of a dozen sheep down to the small quay and, one by one, threw them into the water. They struggled some when he picked them up, but once they were in the water, he had difficulty luring them out. The reason he did this we never knew for sure, but we suspected that it was their daily bath, tick control, perverse shepherdship, or none of the above.

Another sight we enjoyed was two cows in a caique (a small boat about 40 feet long and used for light interisland transport and fishing). They were apparently bound for another island and seemed unperturbed by the fact that they were on an incredibly small boat and about to venture out on the sea. They quietly munched hay as they awaited the return of the skipper. Nancy hurried over and took a picture of this absurd situation because she knew that she would be unable to describe it properly, and if she did, no one would believe her.

The village of Skhinoussa was about one-half kilometer up on the crest of the island. Many villages on these islands were built this way because they were more easily defended in ancient times. We trudged up the hill, planning on an evening meal at the rumored restaurant. It was there, and the young proprietor spoke some English. Along with our meal we ordered a bottle of wine which he brought immediately.

An old man, the only other occupant of the restaurant, smiled and made a few remarks in Greek to us. We offered him some of our wine. He joined us at our table and we chatted for about an hour. Neither of us understood a word spoken by the other, but through pantomime, etc. we spent a very pleasant hour with him. The young proprietor told us the restaurant was owned by the old man who was his father. His father, he said, just enjoyed talking with the customers and he was especially glad to meet us Americans. Being unable to speak the language was a handicap—not a deterrent.

We left Skhinoussa in a flat calm, but once out on the open sea we welcomed back the meltemi and finally dropped anchor in Amorgas' main harbor in the early afternoon. After a few days of exploring Amorgas, Nancy returned to the States and was replaced by Reinhold and Lois.

Reinhold is preparing to retire to a life such as ours and had sailed with me many times in the past. We did some more exploring of Amorgas which included the cliff-hanging abbey mentioned earlier and the main village which was, as you might expect, on the top of the hill. This village was probably the most quintessential of all that we had seen. A road led up to it and terminated on a steep slope that had a paved level spot of possibly one acre. Here the trucks off-loaded their cargo onto donkeys for their trip into the village. The village itself had winding streets with archways, steps, and tiny plazas filled with flowers.

From Amorgas we sailed on to Kos with a stop at Levithia. We had some pretty good sailing for a change, but we were getting out of the meltemi area. At Levithia, the harbor was totally deserted except for a crudely lettered sign that pointed up a path and that read "Disco 1 km."

At Kos, however, we enjoyed a feast of ruins, antiquities, and history. Kos was the island of Socrates. We walked under the tree, very old and supported with timbers, where he was supposed to have lectured to his students. We taxied out to Esclepia, the site of one of the world's first hospitals and tasted the supposedly curative waters. We climbed the walls of an ancient Crusader castle that guarded the harbor and that was still in excellent shape. We wandered through portions of the town where excavations had exposed the ancient city, its walls now only two to four feet high, but its beautiful tile floors still intact. By the time we reached Kos, we were getting a little inured to ruins, but Kos impressed us. It was there also that I got into the ferry's slip by mistake and had to dive to free the prop.

Our next stop was Turkey and the city of Bodrum. We had a fine sail almost all the way across, a distance of 30 to 40 kilometers, but then the wind died and we tried to motor. The engine died also. Reinhold and I performed emergency surgery and soon had it going. Hence, on into Bodrum. As we neared the harbor, the huge castle of St. Peter dominated the approach. This very well-built and well-preserved monolithic structure was built in the 15th century by the Knights of Rhodes Crusaders. It now houses two fine museums, several shady gardens, shops, and a restaurant, and, of course, lots of echoing hallways, parapets, moats, gates, and towers.

We went into the marina in the harbor and then off to our first brush with Turkish customs. Four hours later, thoroughly exhausted, we were officially checked into the country. We did not get good reports on Bodrum as a place to spend the winter, so we rented a car and the four of us drove the 100 kilometers north to Kusadasi to have a close look at that marina. It was clean, new, and had all the amenities and, in addition, a bar and restaurant. We reserved a place, made a down payment, and returned to Bodrum, sidetracking to Ephesus for a little sight-seeing.

We were rewarded to find the site of Ephesus well

preserved. We wandered for a couple of hours through the marbled streets, peered into doors and windows (or where they used to be), visited the bordello (no windows), and the library whose magnificent facade had been carefully restored in its entirety. Wheel tracks were worn in the marble slabs of the streets, from chariots, I'm sure, and the side streets marched up the hill to the villas of the ancient rich. The amphitheater was the largest we had seen, including that in Rome. It is still used today for summer performing arts events and ceremonies.

St. Paul said of Ephesus, "Is there a greater city?" It was once a seaport, but it silted in and now is several kilometers from the Aegean Sea. Archeologists believe that this is the city's third site, its having been moved twice before because of silting.

We returned to Bodrum and Reinhold and Lois prepared to depart. The plan had been for us to sail them over to Kos where they could get a plane to Athens and home. Then we would have a nice sail back. When this agenda was made known to the customs people, we were informed that there was no way we could just simply do that. We would have to check out of Turkey completely, check into Greece completely, and then return and check back into Turkey completely. This dampened our enthusiasm considerably since that would have made a two-day trip out of an afternoon's pleasant sail. Plan B was then executed, which consisted of Reinhold and Lois traveling by ferry to Kos. The ferry captain of the small (40 foot) ferry also took their passports and cleared them out with dispatch, another point in favor of Plan B.

The next day we visited the site of one of the seven ancient wonders of the world, the tomb of Masolus. This and the Temple of Artemis, at Ephesus, another of the seven wonders, illustrate how rich in history is this center of the dawning of civilization on the west coast of Turkey.

We laid in a few supplies and left the next day for Kusadasi, planning a leisurely trip—but we had only just got outside the harbor when I remembered that we had not picked up our trip log. The purpose of this document was obscure but we were told that we must have it when we checked into any harbor. Being totally intimidated by Turkish customs, we turned around and went back into the harbor and dropped our anchor. Expecting to be back soon, we still hoped to make the small bay that was our objective before dinner. Two hours later as the sun was settling on the rim of the western hills, I returned, thoroughly frazzled. I had gone to several offices that I had visited before but no one knew what I was talking about until I got to the harbormaster's office. He said that I must go back to one of the offices I had just left where no one knew what I wanted. There I had to await an official who finally returned, walked over to the file, pulled out my trip log, and handed it to me with a huge smile. His English being minimal, I decided not to ask him why one of his assistants couldn't have done this an hour before. I had to then take it back to the harbormaster who stamped it with a great flourish and wished me a pleasant voyage.

Please understand, the Turkish officials were not surly, they wanted very much to help you, but they dared not buck the system. There, as in the rest of the world, civil service consists of having a great reverence for rules and regulations and NEVER sticking your neck out.

The next day we made it to a bay that looked attractive on the charts and which had good protection from the northern winds of the meltemi. We really were out of their influence, but I still felt intimidated by their threat.

The bay turned out to be one of the five top anchorages in all of our cruising to date. It was a good-sized bay and we had it nearly to ourselves. At the head of it stood a small village with its mosque and minaret. We anchored about a kilometer away in front of a grove of trees. Having finished a light supper, we sipped a small sherry and watched a farmer herding a dozen cows along the beach toward the barn for their evening milking. The bells on their collars were most pleasant to our ears. Then the cry of the muezzin floated over the water as he called the faithful to their evening prayers. I knew nothing of his piousness, but his voice was beautiful. The breeze rustled in the trees and the sun dimmed to a brilliant orange. This is what cruising is all about!

That part of the Turkish west coast had many small islands and small bays and some big bays with smaller bays around them. It looked like, and was, a marvelous cruising ground. Many, many anchorages beckoned us but the weather was getting chilly and we really didn't have a positive location for the winter, so we bypassed most of them to make a steady 20 or 30 miles a day north.

We are now in the marina. After a few days of doubt about whether they could find a place for us, another American boat left and we moved into their slip and then asked permission to stay there for the winter.

There are probably 20 or 30 boats here belonging to cruisers and some will leave to spend the winter at their homes, but most, I hope, will stay. In the meantime, we will be wondering what you are doing and how the holidays are treating you. We hope that this Christmas you will be blessed and surrounded by love, as are we.

    Love,
            Paul & Emily

14

Kusadasi,
Turkey
March 18, 1988

Dear Friends,

I thought you might be interested in what it was like to spend a winter on a boat in a strange land. You are already familiar with our experience in New Zealand, but remember, "down under" it was summer when we spent the winter there. In Kusadasi, on the west coast of Turkey, it was winter, but it was, as usual, a mild one. The reason we wintered in Turkey was that the northern Med was no place to be from November to April because of storms, rain, and, occasionally, snow. The southern Med might have been nice but the nations there were poor, accommodations were terrible and the population, especially Libya, downright unfriendly. The result was that all summer we kept asking those cruisers we met, "Where are you spending the winter?" Many put their boats up "on the hard" (ground) wherever they were and went home. These were usually Europeans who still maintained their homes and cruised only eight or nine months of the year. This was also true of many of the boats in Kusadasi, but they had a choice in that they could leave their boats in the water or have them set out on the hard. Those of us who truly lived aboard and had no other home had to find a nice, modern marina where we could have electricity, water, showers, and laundry. At that moment, Turkey was the most popular with us "live-aboards" as the government had built a number of new marinas and did not charge the exorbitant rates that are found on the French Riviera, and in Italy and Spain.

There was much socializing between the boats and soon we knew everyone of the 30 or 40 who were there. We came from six or eight countries and English was the common language, but several non-English speakers seemed to be enjoying their stay and mingled quite freely. We developed a few friendships a little closer than others, but generally there was absolutely no cliquishness. Also, it should be mentioned that the marina personnel were outstanding and worked very hard to help us enjoy our stay there. They threw one big party at a downtown restaurant which was attended by all the workers and live-aboards. We ate, drank, danced, and were entertained by a belly dancer. We learned to dance the mid-eastern dances and we witnessed one amusing incident in which the men danced with other men. One Canadian woman found herself frequently separated from her husband as a Turkish man injected himself between them. She had to forcefully let him know that she was her husband's partner, by golly!

What did we do all winter? Well, let's start with Thanksgiving. When we first arrived at the marina, we were met by a fellow American who, among other things, suggested that cruisers who were docked at the marina had a big Thanksgiving affair planned. "Count us in," we enthusiastically responded. "Just tell us what we can do to help!" As the day approached, we got only vague responses from him. Worried, Emily and I started from scratch. We contacted all six of the American boats. As "T" day edged closer, one after another, the Americans dropped out. The day before Thanksgiving, one of the Americans was diagnosed as hepatitic. That left just two boats, us and a Hawaiian boat. We switched the dinner from turkey (the bird, readily available in Turkey, and why not?) to a couple of chickens, and changed the location from the marina meeting room to our boat. We also swore in a couple of Brits as temporary Americans, but only after they had solemnly sworn never again to refer to us Americans as "You people from the colonies." The cooperative meal was most delicious!

As the weather grew colder, we frequently lit the cabin heater during the day and used the electric heater to chase the chill in the morning. Our folding bicycles proved to be a valuable asset as downtown Kusadasi was about a kilometer from the marina. Each trip to town was an exciting experience as we dodged people in the streets and were threatened repeatedly by speeding motorists. You see, transportation was not as simple as it was in the U.S. People walked in the streets and shared them with the motorists. The sidewalks were used for other things, such as the displaying of wares by the merchants, locations for tables for small restaurants, the piling of construction materials and, of course, for parking. There was apparently no intention of reserving the sidewalks for pedestrians. It was just as well. They weren't very wide anyhow, and were non-existent in many places. Incidentally this was as true in Paris and the rest of Europe as it was in Kusadasi.

The Turks drove somewhat the same way as the Mexicans. They only used two controls: the accelerator and the horn. To complicate the process there were two and four-wheeled wagons pulled by small donkeys. Some times the donkeys were burdened and led, and occasionally ridden, by their owners. The riders looked monumental on the mount as he or she rode serenely down the street on the back of a beast only slightly larger than a large dog. Old dobbin had been largely replaced by tractors for pulling the regular, four-wheeled, rubber-tired farm wagon, thus proving that gasoline was cheaper than oats.

The big day in Kusadasi was Friday, Market Day! The marketeers were not only local people bringing their produce to market, but also consisted of wandering merchants who took their wares to five or six markets each week on different days. Emily always looked forward to Friday and took her "granny cart" with her so that she could bring back more vegetables and fruits. In the market, in literally acres of stalls, you could find almost any kind of merchant: the ironmonger, the brass smith, the cloth merchant, the potter, the basket weaver, the rope-maker, the fisherman and, of course, always the ubiquitous seller of watches and costume jewelry. Of greatest interest and by far the most colorful were the fruit and vegetable stalls. There, piled in colorful mounds were the most beautiful, plumpest and juiciest fruits and vegetables that we had ever seen anywhere! Emily browsed through this section in a daze of pure ecstasy! For accent there was the "dry merchant" with his open bags of beans, lentils, rices and grains. Alongside might be a savory spice merchant with his heaps of aromatic and colorful materials.

Meanwhile, back at the marina, the yachting community filled the time between major events with a busy social schedule. Almost everyone had almost everyone else over for tea, coffee, cocktails or dinner. A lot of time was spent at the tavern that was almost exclusively for the use of the yachties. Lots of meeting were conducted there.

The next major event was Christmas. This was a joint effort with first mates Emily, Pat, and Carol playing leading roles. It truly was a remarkably well-coordinated and successful event according to the 19 who participated. We bought a couple of turkeys, Pat stuffed them, and they were roasted in the marina kitchen oven. Everything else came from the yachts. The decorations were homemade (Turkey being an Islamic country it was virtually impossible to find standard tinsel, baubles, etc.) but colorful and clever. On the table were green bay branches, a sprig of which was hung in our cabin and flavored an occasional stew. We sang carols, and talked and ate—and ate. The affair was slightly dimmed by the fact that the other half of the cruisers had, unbeknownst to us, organized their own party and held it in a downtown restaurant which had provided all the food, decorations, etc. I don't think they had half the fun we did.

For example, after Pat had stuffed the turkeys, a couple of us men carried them over to the compound kitchen where we had arranged to have them baked. The day before the women had talked through an interpreter to the chef to see if we could bake some potatoes at the same time. He replied, "Of course, no problem. We will bake them while the turkeys are boiling." Boiling? Turkeys? The women blanched, the faces of the men turned red. It took us about 20 minutes to get across that the American way was to bake the turkeys for a long time in a moderate oven. The birds would be stuffed. He said, "Not necessary, I will be glad to make the stuffing separately." He just didn't get the idea for about 20 minutes.

Please understand, he did want so much to help us and to save us work.

He finally said to just bring them over in the morning and he would do whatever we wanted. We did this and I decided to check on things a half-hour later. He smiled and said that the turkeys would be finished in a half-hour. We had calculated that it would take about six hours at a slow bake. I turned the oven down to half what it was and raced over to consult with the ladies. We checked and basted and then checked again in one hour and decided the turkeys were done, but we couldn't tell how well. Everything, of course, turned out okay but we wondered what would have happened if we had just handed them to him and said, "Please cook them."

Incidentally, the management brought over a music system, some decorations, plates and cutlery, and we used their assembly hall normally reserved for big shots. They did try hard to make us feel welcome.

The other group had a good time, too, and we vowed to get together for New Year's Eve. We learned later that they had 40 or 50 at the celebration, held in the same place as our Christmas party. In the meantime, we had signed up for a conducted tour of Egypt and spent New Year's Eve on a boat on the Nile.

Let me commence this episode by saying to one and all that this is the only way to go to Egypt. I do not like the country and I do not like the people. You can do nothing without the payment of baksheesh. Beggars are everywhere, as are the intrusive and offensive street merchants. I was cheated out of $150 in a sly con game by one of the leading banks of Egypt. If you think I am bigoted, go there first and then judge me.

Yes, we did see the Pyramids, the Sphinx and the huge temples that were two or three thousand years old. We visited the tomb of Tutankhamen and the Aswan Dam. The museum at Cairo is almost unbelievable. It seemed that more than half of the exhibits were artifacts from King Tut's tomb. When you think that this was the only tomb that was left untouched by grave robbers, and that he was only a minor Pharaoh, you realize that thousands of acres of floor space would have been needed if the grave robbers had not been so successful.

New Year's Eve was spent on the riverboat that was our home as we traveled up the river from Luxor to Aswan. This was almost dream-like and I understood why Cleopatra was so successful in her seduction of Antony. We slowly moved up the river between banks where little had changed since the time of the Pharaohs. Camels, water buffalo, and donkeys still seemed to be the major form of transportation in the fields. Several times we saw water being pumped up into the fields by a water buffalo who plodded in circles lifting water into a ditch with earthen jars. Mud huts appeared to be the major type of buildings and, in many places, the deep green of the sugar cane, cotton, and other crops contrasted starkly with the clearly visible tan of the desert in the distance.

We stopped at villages along the way to visit temples, tombs, and village tourist-type shops. We learned to read a few hieroglyphics. Our guide was fluent in English and hieroglyphics appeared to be his hobby. He was proud of his country's antiquities.

The group consisted of about eight Turkish couples who seemed more interested in shopping than sightseeing, a French couple, a Japanese family, and an American couple (us). The food was excellent and the chef did his best to cater to our tastes. The boat sponsored a New Year's Eve party with hats, favors, serpentine, and a glass of champagne for each of us. After midnight, the crew brought out drums and cymbals and danced for us and soon had us out on the floor to perform their native dances. I must have acquitted myself reasonably well. Near the end of the trip, we were having an elegant dinner on a Cairo riverboat and were entertained by a belly dancer. After her major dance she toured the tables getting men to get up and dance with her. The Turks in our party thought it would be great fun for the American man to dance with her. With some urging I did so—so now I am probably the only guy you know who has danced with an Egyptian belly dancer on a barge on the river Nile.

Do not misunderstand, you should visit Egypt. There is, there, a marvelous record of a great and glorious age. That age is past. Egypt now is a miserable, tiny country with almost universal poverty, tawdry hovels, haphazard streets teeming with people, all of whom are "working" each other or the tourists. Their currency is worthless (outside the country) and their leaders try to grapple with world problems while making little attempt to solve those at home. The Nile is a rich national resource and the export of agricultural products is the Egyptian's principal source of wealth—except, of course, the tourists who come to see the monuments to Egypt's past glory. Yes, by all means go, but only on a guided tour. Our guide protected us as much as possible from the seamy side, but we still saw enough of it to shudder, thinking about what might have been had he not been there.

Another major event at the marina was Kid's Day. It all started rather innocently as a small group along the north quay decided to adopt a yellow dog that was heavily pregnant. They planned a fund-raising event to get the bitch, whose name was Oscar, spayed and provide shots for her, the puppies, and Toby, the suspected father. (When the puppies were born there was no doubt about it.) Toby was an Anatolian guard dog who had been appointed as official pontoon guard dog by the yachting communities. A house was built for him by one of the boats and several of us saw that he was well fed. When we bore the major responsibility, my supper often awaited the completion of Toby's meal. Toby was very arthritic and we wanted to do something about that, too.

The story of how this got involved with kids begins with the entry of a British gentleman who said, "Why waste the effort on a couple of dogs? Why not involve the boy's orphan school in nearby Aydin?" It seemed reasonable, so a lot of fund-raising events were held and a chart was kept in the tavern to show our progress toward our goal. There were dart contests, bridge parties, rummage sales, bingo games, and video movies. A rather impressive sum was raised from the yachties and, even more, the camaraderie and cohesiveness of the community grew stronger. In the meantime, we discussed and developed activities to entertain the boys when they arrived.

They arrived on the appointed day, 150 strong, in two buses. It was terrifying, but we were ready with all kinds of games and activities. The three most popular activities were the ferry boat ride, the water-bombing contest (where wet sponges were thrown at a human target whose feet are clamped in a stock), and, Emily's contribution, face painting. Emily stood by her table with her own face painted and was studiously ignored. I went out into the crowd and strong-armed one of the older boys who seemed to be a leader of sorts. We finally convinced him to give it a try. From then on, until we closed shop, Emily never rested.

We, of course, fed them with popcorn and soft drinks during the day and hamburgers and roast lamb and chicken for the evening meal. We had a lot of lamb left over, a lot of chicken, but guess what? No hamburger!

The boys in turn, put on a little show for us with songs and imitations (one did Elvis Presley). None of them spoke English but they mingled at the various tables. As I've said before, language is not a barrier, just a mild handicap. We were told later that the boys all said that it was the best time that they had ever had in their lives. The yachties walked around for several days with a glow of fulfillment in their hearts.

One cool but sunny January day we went to see some camels wrestle. This was a big event in that part of Turkey and fans and competitors came from far parts of the realm. I will describe the whole ceremony as there was more ceremony than action in this contest. The camels in this case were not beasts of burden but fighting camels—all males. A very demur female was led around the ring and then the males were paired off. A lot of time elapsed between contests, but when they faced off, the beasts pushed and shoved and tried to bite each other's ankles. This process continued while "judges" crouched around giving points to this or that beast. After a while the camels were forced apart and led out of the arena. Later, the winning camel, already heavily laden with rugs from past encounters, was led across the arena with his newly won rug draped carelessly over his back. Later, during lunch, we talked with one of the owners and petted his huge beast. He was very proud of his camel's accomplishments and also of the two bags of wool that the animal produced each year. The wool grows only on the chest of the males. Now I know where camel-hair coats come from.

    The expedition to the camel matches was organized by the manager of the marine supply store at the marina. He knew little about the point system used for judging, but the real pleasure in the day was watching the crowd there in the coliseum at Ephesus where the event is held each year. Picture the huge, sloping hills covered with thousands of people and at lunch as they prepared the shish kebabs, the smoke of small fires drifting up and away. There were no seats, just the grassy slope. Down on the flat of the playing field, smoky fires at lunch time sent up a tantalizing aroma. We sampled the wares of a teriyaki shish kebab vendor and enjoyed a flavor that lives in our memories yet today. A small musical group struck up some tunes that soon had some men dancing as the crowd cleared a space for them. They were great! Much better than I.

    Is that all we did in the winter? No, those were the high spots. We toured the land, visited antiquities, and worked on the boat. Emily painted, I tinkered, and we shopped in Izmir, the third largest city in Turkey. We even went to Istanbul and visited all the grandeur of this ancient capital of the Ottoman Empire. It was there that I visited my first Turkish bath. Later, I went again in Kusadasi. And, would you believe it? Several ladies from the marina organized a lady's day at the Turkish bath in Kusadasi. I also had the job of dealing with <u>customs</u>. This is underlined because it takes so much of one's time. That is a factor that you must put into any project equation here in Turkey. In total, we imported five packages into Turkey during our winter there and I estimated that three full weeks of my time was spent waiting and running about trying to get the packages through customs.

    At the moment we are cozy in our boat, the cabin heater radiates gently, and this Sunday has been devoted to sewing, painting, and writing. All this as a cold wind howls down from the steppes of Russia and hurls itself across the marina. The rigging shrieks around us but we are content and happy. We hope you are.

    Love,
        Paul and Emily

15

On board Golden Bell
Somewhere in Turkey
May 22, 1988

Dear Friends,

Spring came to the west coast of Turkey at last. The sun was warm and the breezes were gentle and, one by one, our cruising friends departed the marina for the seasonal cruise. All of us were weary of the civilization of the marina, town, and, yes, even the social life that gave us so much pleasure during the winter. Our cruising friends were all marvelous people and we felt that we had made life-long friends there. But we longed for the remote anchorages and the small, unspoiled villages and bays that proliferated on the Turkish coast. We had to cruise the area then because the isolated bays were fast filling with high-rise condos. The quaint streets and markets were filling with rug and brass merchants. It was sad to us, but it was a harvest of gold to which the Turks have, perhaps rightly, dedicated themselves.

From Kusadasi we could fan out in three directions for the start of our cruising season. North to Istanbul and the Black Sea, out (west) to the Greek islands, and south along the scalloped Turkish coast, Cyprus, the Arab nations fronting on the Mediterranean, and Israel. We went south, for reasons that will be clear, and chose St. Paul's Harbor as our first destination. Two of our closer friends, on Malgre Toute, decided to meet us there the first night, although they were going west.

This little anchorage was totally isolated and had the temerity to call itself a harbor only because the great St. Paul, the Apostle, was purported to have stopped there on his way to Ephesus in order to rest his rowers.

We anchored in two meters of water that was crystal clear. The anchoring process consisted of dropping the anchor in a likely spot where we would have adequate room to swing with the wind and where the anchor would dig in and hold. The first attempt failed and when we attempted to set the anchor by backing off under power, it dragged along the bottom. So, we gathered in the anchor line and Emily carefully searched out a sandy spot and dropped the anchor in it and the anchor held.

We were soon joined by Jay and Miri on Malgre Toute. Most of us cruising couples were known by our first names and the name of our boat. For example, we were

Paul and Emily of Golden Bell. Few knew that our last name is Keller, nor could we give you the last name of many of our close cruising friends, although we could tell you the name of their boat.

Malgre Toute also had a little difficulty setting their anchor. But, they were soon settled in, dinghy launched, and exploring as we were doing. We spent the afternoon on the small island that sheltered the harbor. Emily specializes in flowers, especially tiny ones. I specialize in views and geology. Our expedition uncovered a tiny blue orchid which transported Emily into ecstasy, while I drank deeply of the lonely isolation. Our isolation was fleeting, however, as a small, open fishing boat put-putted onto the harbor at dusk. Jay knew some Turkish and attempted to negotiate a fish or lobster for us. They wanted whiskey, but we cautiously denied having any. They had nothing to trade, anyway. The fishermen (one of the three was a woman) settled in for the night and this caused a little apprehension on our part, as they were a scruffy lot. The next morning they put-putted out of sight, leaving me feeling a little guilty for having been suspicious of their intentions.

After waving good-bye to our friends on Malgre Toute, we set a course for the next cape, our objective for the night being a small harbor around a second cape. The haze that blankets the Med almost all year kept us from seeing the shore only five miles away. We knew at all times where we were thanks to our Loran, which you may remember is a position locator based on radio signals. It was functioning well so Emily resumed her position as chief officer in charge of dots. Dot-making is the process of marking your position on a chart, updating it every half hour or so. It is fascinating to watch this orderly progression of dots across the chart toward your objective, especially when you can see nothing but haze. After we reached our objective, a slight breeze sprang up so we hoisted sail and had a fine sail eastward along the coast. We had one anxious moment when the bottom suddenly came up from no soundings to five meters in less than 30 seconds. No sounding means that the water is so deep that our echo sounder, with a limit to its range of 50 meters, does not indicate a solid object below us.

The chart had indicated that this spot was covered with only five meters of water. I didn't care. When I'm three miles offshore, I don't like to have the nearest land only five meters away, especially when my first mate is screaming, "I can see bottom!" So. We swerved out into deeper water.

A meter, for the benefit of those who live in the only country still using the length of a long-dead king's foot as the unit of measure, is about 39 inches---just think of it as about a yard. I wonder how much longer the U.S. will continue to suffer the inconvenience of the English system? England, itself, you know, is nearly converted to the metric system.

We made our objective harbor in mid-afternoon. We entered the harbor in a strong cross-breeze and then went back out again. Emily circled the boat while I assembled our 100 lb. fisherman's anchor which we carried disassembled in the bilge. With this dropped in the harbor, we felt rather secure from dragging anchors, but we soon set another good sand anchor in addition, just in case one of them decided to drag.

The wind increased in strength, and since the harbor was unprotected from the wind by buildings or trees, we decided to post an anchor watch. This meant that one of us had to be awake at all times, checking frequently to determine whether the anchor was dragging or not. About 2:00 a.m., the wind died and we slept soundly until morning. This night, of course, was in stark contrast to the idyllic night before.

There were also some annoying and frustrating moments. We had had no mail for several weeks and had telexed our secretarial service to send our mail to Bodrum—a new, modern harbor where we expected to be in ten days. When we arrived there, we found out that the management had returned it the day after it had arrived over a week before. His excuse? Our yacht was not on his list of residents. Clearly marked on the packet were the words "Yacht in Transit, Please Hold For Arrival."

This was a devastating experience. We told the manager, who spoke good English, that all over the Pacific and the Mediterranean marina managers and harbormasters held mail for transients like ourselves. We had not thought that in this popular cruising area there would be a manager so insensitive as to not do this for cruisers who brought large amounts of foreign currency and goodwill into their country. We telexed the secretarial service to re-send the package to American Express on the island of Rhodes in Greece.

We are now in Marmaris, just a short distance from Rhodes and we have telephoned and telexed the Amex office there repeatedly. No one answers the phone. The telex machine acknowledged that the message was received in Rhodes, so we waited another 24 hours and no answer came. And we will wait another 24 hour in the hope that someone will look at the telex or answer the phone. We do not want to go there if there is no mail. If we do go, it will probably be by ferry. You who live in the U. S. cannot appreciate the fine service that you get from your post office and telephone company—overnight mail, directory assistance, lots of long-distance lines, and help from friendly and sympathetic operators and clerks who care about your needs. As I write this, we have decided to wait another 24 hours and then do something drastic, even if it is wrong.

Yes, there are problems, but that is a part of this life. One of the problems that we don't have is boredom. For example, to get to this harbor on the south coast of Turkey, we had a marvelous sail. We were having so much fun on a broad reach, which is Golden Bell's best point of sail, that we just kept going and soon lost touch with land. After three hours of glorious "bone in her teeth" sailing (a term used because the white, foaming curl of the water at the bow resembles a dog with a white bone in its mouth), we tacked back into shore, only to discover that we could not identify any of the landmarks. We kept on going, however, and I turned on the Loran. That part of the Med had weak Loran signals, but we got one good fix which showed that we had passed our harbor entrance by about three miles. We dropped the sails and motored back and, with difficulty in the haze, finally found the entrance. On the chart, there was a light indicated at the entrance, but we had passed within one-half mile of it without being able to see it. The Turks and many countries around the Med, do not see the importance of easily visible day marks such as are common in the more advanced countries. This light was on a spidery tower standing against a neutral background, was dark in color, and was only about three meters high. In the haze it blended in beautifully with the rocky background. Perhaps the most famous of the lights is the Eddystone Light in the English channel. Its candy stripes and wide girth are visible for many miles, even when the haze is troublesome.

There were many more delightful anchorages on this beautiful southern Turkish coast. One in particular that will stay in our memories forever was Buyuk Liman. This was the site of the ancient city of Knidos, renowned in its day for two things: its spectacular statue of Aphrodite, the goddess of love, and its scientist, Eudoxos. Eudoxos is considered one of the founding fathers of Greek astronomy and geometry, but unlike Pythagoras, never had a theorem named after him.

At one time, Knidos was a proud and bustling city of several thousand people who became enriched because they were on the direct trade route from the Orient to the prosperous southern European countries. Now there is only a jumble of squared stones, a few columns, and an overgrown theater where a few goats browse, and one forlorn tavern that awaits the coming of the chartered tourist boats that drop in and out of the harbor. It is bare and lifeless, but teeming with the ghosts of the past. Every time we visit one of these 2,000-or-more-year-old ruins of once prosperous cities, we would be willing to trade our lives, fortunes, and sacred honor, in reverse order of course, for one time-machine trip into the past to view the color and glamour that must have been here. It also causes one to wonder what will be left on Manhattan Island in 2,000 years, or on the Thames River or Tokyo Bay.

We also dropped anchor in a little harbor called Asin Liman. It was small, but had been the site of a bustling town of Iassus and its principal export was salted fish. The story is told that once, during a performance at the theater, the gong which signaled the start of the fish market was sounded. The entire audience, all but one, hurried out immediately to the market. The remaining man was deaf, but as soon as someone explained to him why the rest of the audience had deserted, he, too, shuffled off.

The ruins of this charming small city had been partially excavated by an Italian group. Most of the excavations and restoration had been done by archeologists with funds from countries all over the world. In more recent times, an olive grove had been planted over the ruins, resulting in a shady, park-like setting. Cows grazed contentedly among the trees and temples. We walked down what had once been a broad avenue leading to an elaborate square that had been excavated completely. Many of the fluted columns had been set up on their bases. These were the remains of what must have been a magnificent temple to Zeus.

We then climbed a low hill to the quite complete remains of a Crusader castle built by the Knights of St. John. On the grassy hillock where it stood, the ground was strewn with potsherds, and cows and donkeys grazed and stood in the shade of the olive trees. Descending to the harbor, we examined a fort guarding the entrance which was built by the Byzantines. It was in remarkably good repair as was the old quay still visible under a few inches of water. As we continued on to our starting point, we passed a remarkable, almost whole small theater and startled a donkey out of its shade. I stood on the stage floor and delivered a few lines of Lincoln's Gettysburg Address to a wildly cheering phantom audience. A jackass trumpeted mournfully in the distance. We decided we would keep our sacred honor since, with a little imagination, we had just purchased a voyage into the past.

    I am continuing this a couple of weeks later in Larnaca, Cyprus. The above was written before leaving Marmaris. While there, through the good offices of a nice young man in a travel agency, we discovered that Amex had changed hands and had moved to a new agency. After some prompting, they telexed that there was no mail for us there, either. Later, our secretarial service said that they had never received the telex from the Bodrum marina to send the mail to Rhodes. Inured by now to this sort of thing, we resignedly gave up and planned our crossing to Cyprus. Our plan to go there was the result of contacting our old friends from the South Pacific, Don and Rhoda on Sunchaser. We knew that this spring they would have crossed the Indian Ocean and would be somewhere in the Red Sea, so we tried to contact them on the ham radio through the U.K. Net. This is a daily gathering of hams at 8:00 a.m. and is supervised by a man in England.

    One morning in Kusadasi, we were eating breakfast and had forgotten to turn on the ham radio, when our friend, Jay, who is also a ham, burst onto the boat and yelled, "Turn on your rig quickly, there is a man in Egypt trying to contact you on the U.K. Net!" To turn on the rig, get it tuned, and wait for it to warm up would have taken several minutes, so instead I rushed over to Malgre Toute. When it was proper, I said to the U.K. control, "This is N7IIR, I understand KA4IQQ has been trying to reach me."

    "Right," he said. "KA4IQQ, are you there?"

    Then Don's voice came out, "This is KA4IQQ, I

sure am. Hello, Paul, where shall we go?"

I suggested a frequency and we moved off the Net frequency. After a few minutes of catching up on each other's movements and plans, we agreed to meet on the island of Cyprus, port of Larnaca on or near June 1. When we arrived at Marmaris it was very late in May.

The two or three-day passage to Cyprus ordinarily would have been no problem for us. But Emily was recovering from a bout of asthma and not quite up to the three-day two-night crossing. We found help in a young couple from San Diego who were on a circumnavigation in a 24-foot motorless boat. They readily agreed to accompany us even though Karen was seven months pregnant. Mike was a superb sailor and made Golden Bell perform better than ever under the old skipper. We ticked off miles rapidly under fresh breezes most of the way. Karen and Emily stood one night-watch each and Mike and I two. These got us through the critical darkness hours in safety. It was a comfort to have Karen and Mike's experience aboard.

The person on watch must sweep the horizon each few minutes and watch for freighters. We who put to sea in small boats have little fear of sharks, whales, or storms. The one thing we universally dread is a collision with a freighter. They are usually on auto-pilot, the crew are low-paid Orientals, and the officers are usually below or drunk. My guess is that only one out of three maintain a proper watch for small boats. When you realize that they can come up from the horizon and be alongside in 15 minutes, you can understand the need for a continuous watch. It is possible, by reading the lights of a freighter, to determine its approximate course. If it looks possible that you could both arrive at the same place at the same time, i.e. a collision is possible, the person on watch will start avoidance action, turn on all lights, etc. That is why it was a comfort to have an experienced crew onboard. The skipper, me, did not have to be called for every light sighted.

Needless to say, we made it safely to Cyprus, rendezvoused with Sunchaser, and are now getting our mail. We will leave here after July 1 and go rather rapidly to the western Mediterranean. We hope to get in a month or so of cruising around southern Spain before going to Gibraltar to prepare for our Atlantic crossing in December from the Canaries. We will be joining 100 or so other cruisers in a "race" to Barbados. We will then be back in our home hemisphere for a change.

We hope you have a great summer and, in the meantime, keep well and happy.

Love,
        Paul and Emily

CYPRUS

16

Alicante,
Spain
August 30, 1988

Dear Friends,

    This letter might be entitled the "Mis-adventures" rather than the further "Adventures" of Paul and Emily. The dominating factor is a storm that changed our schedule and resulted in some unplanned adventures rather than those we had planned. Let me interject the truism that in the life aboard a cruising sailboat, one does not "plan" in the positive and detailed way that you might in a more orderly life. Storms, breakdowns, cantankerous officials, palace coups, and all sorts of things can change your plans. So you just "go with the flow," as I believe the young generation would put it.

But let's put the storm in its logical place and start with a very delightful month spent on the island of Cyprus. Cyprus is the third largest island in the Mediterranean and lies in a strategic spot at the eastern end of the Med. In ancient days, it was the crossroads for commercial traffic from three continents. The Suez Canal has not lessened its glory, but it does not thrive as it did of yore. It now lies in a state of tension resulting from the invasion of the Greek island in 1974 by the Turkish army. The northern part is not accessible from the southern, Greek, part. Fertile coastal plains surround a mountainous interior.

We went to Cyprus to meet our friends from the South Pacific, Don and Rhoda of Sunchaser. It was quite a thrill to enter the harbor at Larnaca and see the familiar shape and yellow stripe and covering of Sunchaser. We immediately started to make plans and Don and I resumed our long-standing feud about who was the better cribbage player. We rented a small car and drove on a tour of the island. Of the driving, I remember starkly the terror I felt while Don was driving us on a very narrow, precipitous mountain road. The other time was when I was driving and we met a huge semi-truck on a one-lane dirt road. I have been in a lot of the world's mountains, but these were straight up and down. And not a sign of a barricade or safety wall anywhere. To put it mildly, they were challenging—more to nerves than to driving skill.

But tucked away in these mountains were some amazing villages and abbeys. By custom, any abbey will put you up for one night for no charge. Hospitality to the traveler, you know. They used to provide a meal in the morning also, but none of the priests mentioned it to us. We didn't really care, but there was nowhere else to stay and we had brought lots of food with us.

These abbeys were beautiful structures built of the most modern materials. They were manned by priests of the Greek Orthodox Church and were very rich. In one abbey, we were allowed to visit the treasure room where there were many objects of pure gold studded with precious stones. Cyprus, like most Mediterranean countries is afflicted with pervasive poverty and I wondered why the churches should be so rich. I asked. The answer the father gave me was, "Many people dedicate their lands and possessions to the church when they die. A large portion of the land on Cyprus is owned by the churches." I suppose that is a good plan but what about land reform?

We stopped by the side of a pretty, rippling stream and had a marvelous picnic lunch which included sandwiches and watermelon. After lunch, we hiked up a stream on a well-traveled trail to see a waterfall. We also visited a small village built mostly up and down with the streets zigzaging up the hill. Emily grabbed her sketchbook and spent several happy hours there. We stayed in a small hotel of a half-dozen rooms. It was run by two ladies, sisters, I think, one who cooked, the other who ran the rest of it.

"May we get our evening meal here?" Don asked.

"Yes," she answered. Period. No more response.

"Should we look at the menu?" he asked, "or something." This because there were no other guests in the hotel.

She replied with an impish grin, "Dinner will be a

surprise." With this she swept out into the kitchen.

Rhoda said, "I think we will be quite satisfied with what we get tonight."

Emily agreed. After the meal that evening, about five or six courses, as I remember, Paul and Don also agreed.

We drove to Nicosia, the capital city, and saw the checkpoint dividing that city between the Turkish and Greek territory. Passions still run high over this division of the country with politicians making frequent statements which generally exacerbate rather than diminish the problem. Our drive through the countryside between Larnaca and Nicosia revealed one of the reasons this island was impoverished. Much of the way was absolutely sun-baked barren, covered only sparsely with a wiry grass, suitable only for the grazing of goats. However, the government, I presumed, had embarked on a tree-planting program. In many places we saw rows of olive trees that had obviously been planted and seemed to thrive.

Possibly our most memorable experience in Cyprus was attending a performance of *A Midsummer Night's Dream* in an amphitheater that was about 3,500 years old. It was located on a high bluff looking out over the blue sea. To the left, far below, we could see tilled fields green with the summer crops. Before the performance, we wandered through nearby ruins of what once was a great complex of baths, temples, villas, and forums that constituted the rich city-kingdom of Kurion. We had packed a picnic dinner, which we ate, as did many others, sitting on the great stone tiers that rose from the stage in this restored structure. We needed no wine, although we had brought a cold riesling to go with our meal. The heady air and scenery that lay before us were intoxicating enough. Soon the sun touched the horizon and the performance began. It was soon dark and we no longer divided our attention between the play and the scenery. Scenes were changed by changing lights. The rascally Puck was magnificent and the diaphanous fairies danced with exceptional grace. And the delightful ringing poetry of Shakespeare never sounded better than there on that site where Ptolemy, the pot-bellied great-grandfather of Cleopatra, had established this playhouse.

Too soon the month that we had allotted for Cyprus approached an end and we began to make noises about going. We felt that we must be out of the Aegean before July 1 because that is when the meltemi starts to blow. We were not in meltemi country, but we had to cross it before we arrived west of the Peloponnesian peninsula. I think we felt somewhat the way our ancestors did, the ones who had to cross hostile Indian country before arriving in Oregon Territory. We planned to go straight to Crete without stopping, a three-day trip. However, the American community in Cyprus, consisting of six boats, began to talk about a Fourth of July celebration, and it seemed almost un-American to just walk out on it. Besides, the advent of the meltemi is supposed to start on July 1. Sometimes it starts a little earlier, sometimes (possibly this time) a little later. So we stayed.

We planned a regular Fourth of July picnic for the date and we all purchased or manufactured our contributions. We festooned our boats with all the flags we owned. I had four retired U.S. flags, a bunch of courtesy flags and a strip of used-car-lot banners all flying. Most of the boats flew the colorful alphabet of signal flags. We contacted the harbor police for permission to fire some of our outdated flares. It was denied. Someone out at sea might think someone in the harbor needed help, was their reasoning. The picnic started about 5:00 p.m. on the quay in front of the heaviest concentration of U.S. boats with a few tables set up and a grill or two. Soon others of all nationalities brought over casseroles and other food as their contributions. This is sort of standard procedure. You might remember a while back I said that parties were more or less harbor events rather than boat events. Anyway, it turned out to be a smashing event of international flavor. I never knew so many people were so glad we had gained our freedom some 200 years ago. Or maybe cruisers just like parties. We fell into bed rather late that night.

The next morning, as planned, we arose a 8:00 a.m. and got under way. Several, but not many, of the celebrants were on hand to wave good-bye as we motored out of the harbor. Emily, now in good health, was the only crew and the short trip, we hoped, would not upset our biological clocks with the watch standing. We motored almost the length of Cyprus before any wind was available to fill the sails. Then a soft breeze sprang up and, with all sails set, we started our watches for the first night.

We had a great sail almost all the way to Crete, our destination the harbor of Iraklion. We had been in touch with a wonderful French couple, Robert and Susan of Hiawatha of Beaulieu whom we had met in Larnaca. As we approached the eastern coast of Crete, the wind changed and began to "head us" (blow from the direction we wanted to go). We talked to Bob on the ham radio and he told us they had tried unsuccessfully during the day to go between the island of Crete and the island of Kasos. This pass, about 35 miles wide, must be negotiated in order to reach Iraklion on the north coast. It also funnels the northerly winds as they leave the Cyclades and pass on out into the Mediterranean. We learned later that it is called "the Devil's sea" by the local fishermen. You may recall that the meltemi is a northerly wind. Bob said he was going to just wait out the blow in a small harbor on the eastern coast of Crete so we hoped to join him.

We hove-to for the night as we could not make the small harbor before nightfall. A couple of days later Bob made it through to a sheltered bay on the north coast by motor sailing in a rough sea. We tried again and again to break through, but soon the winds became so fierce and the waves so violent that we tried just heaving-to for two days. This was followed by an attempt to sail upwind not to penetrate the pass, but to reach a harbor on the island of Karpathos where we would wait out this meltemi. After all, it couldn't last forever—could it? Karpathos was just a little northeast of Kasos, but we sailed for a day and a half and just couldn't seem to make the last few miles into the harbor. We had tried the engine, but it quit on us and wouldn't start again. We were getting tired. The waves on the Med are short and choppy making the boat move unpleasantly. We had fought this meltemi for six days and there was no sign of let up. We held a council of war. We could go back to Cyprus, downwind. We might make Rhodes, a one-and-a-half-day sail to the northeast. Or we could call for help and get a tow into Karpathos. We elected to surrender and call for help.

I called on all of the emergency channels for help. I was ignored on the VHF, but this is only a short-distance radio. I got on the long-range SSB frequencies. No one, literally no one, answered. This is an international distress frequency that is supposed to be monitored by all ships at sea, all military craft, and all shore coast guard stations. On the ham radio I contacted Bob who was still in the bay on Crete and told him of our plight and our decision. He contacted a friend on a powerboat who was now approaching Rhodes. This marvelous ham then contacted the Rhodes officials on VHF. They alerted the rescue group on Karpathos. After some discussion about our location, relayed through Bob, the wonderful news came through to two tired people: "Stay where you are. A boat is coming out to tow you in to Karpathos."

About an hour later, we saw a fishing boat heading south in toward the shore. We were full of blessed relief when they turned and headed directly for us. Soon they were alongside. It was an ordinary fishing boat. We tossed the deckhand a line while the skipper of the boat did a magnificent job of maneuvering his boat in close. Two hours later, we entered the harbor of Karpathos and safety and, most important to us, relatively calm water.

The end of this story is financial. We approached the negotiations as to fee with some concern, as we had heard stories of outrageous towing fees charged by boat owners who were backed up by the local harbormaster who would not let you leave until the fee was paid. I suggested a figure to the harbormaster who was doing the translating. The fishing captain talked for a few minutes which increased my alarm. I knew and he knew that he was sitting in the controlling position. The harbormaster had told me that we must get things settled before our boat could leave the harbor. The fishing captain told the harbormaster how many days of fishing he had lost and would lose and the great amount of fuel required to tow us back. I countered by saying, "This small sum is all the money I have with me and that is why I offered it. It would leave me with no money to buy food and supplies." It was interesting that we talked only in dollars. The amount in drachmas was never mentioned.

The amount we finally agreed on was double the first offer but a sum I would have gladly agreed to out there in the storm-tossed waves. I think the fisherman was reasonable. He could have demanded five times the amount and the harbormaster would have had no alternative but to impound our boat until it was paid. Incidentally, books and articles tell you to get an agreed-upon figure before you take the line from the rescue boat. A great idea. But we were exhausted. The fisherman spoke no English and I spoke no Greek. So we had to depend on the humanity of humans which, I think, is stronger than the average lawyer would lead you to believe.

We then spent the next couple of weeks trying to punch through the "Devil's sea." We went out of the harbor twice and were turned back by high seas and strong winds. There were a French yacht and an American yacht in the harbor also, for the same reason. They went out on the days that we didn't and tried to gain Iraklion. Each evening they would limp back into the harbor. One day the French boat did not return. We thought that they had lucked out and found a hole in the storm. Five days later they come back into port. They had tried each of the five days and had anchored in a small bay by the airport at the tip of the island for the night.

We gave up! We called a professional delivery service in England and asked them to send a skipper and crew to take our boat to Alicante, Spain. We did this because it was getting late in the season and we had to be in Gibraltar in October to prepare to cross the Atlantic at the proper time with a fleet of other cruisers who traditionally did this each year. Besides, we do not like to rush and face deadlines with no time to spare. We are retired and sailing has got to be fun. We might have made it on our own by going south to a point near the African coast to escape the meltemi, and then sailing non-stop to Spain. Not what we had planned at all. And we would have had precious little time to spend on the Costa del Sol (coast of the sun, or the southern Spanish coast).

In due time, the skipper and his crew arrived in Karpathos and we prepared to turn the boat over to him. He was concerned about a number of items on the boat which he didn't think were up to snuff. Some of the minor things I agreed to, but we had some differences about others. Here we had a strong-willed captain (me) with 25,000 miles of experience, and a professional who was patiently tolerant of the amateur. For another thing, he insisted on being paid in pounds which was impossible there in Karpathos. The single bank had no pounds for sale. I finally got the skipper to agree to take dollars which I had to argue with the bank manager to get.

The manager said, "I have no dollars."

I said, "You have the $4,000 we had wired to your bank. I want them. And don't tell me you don't have them."

After consulting with the head office in Athens, he said, "How much do you want?" The country is glad to take hard currency in, but it is difficult to get them to let it go out. This is true of most of the third and second-world countries. These three strong personalities clashed and sparred for a couple of days but finally things got ironed out.

A surprising window in the wind occurred, so on a moment's notice, Golden Bell, under a new skipper and with the owners acting as crew, departed for Iraklion late one afternoon. We spent the night transiting the "Devil's sea" in a complete calm and under power and arrived in Iraklion the next afternoon. After smoothing over a few more minor incidents we departed on a plane for Scandinavia. I will say little about Scandinavia as it was mostly just touristy stuff.

One vivid memory remains, however. I boarded the plane in Athens during a very hot August day wearing shorts, sandals, and a golf shirt. Emily was similarly burdened. We arrived in Copenhagen on a cool afternoon and I waited shivering for my luggage. But it never appeared on the carousel. Somehow my suitcase got lost and was shipped to Chicago. Emily's case arrived OK.

We went to our hotel and spent the evening on the telephone to SAS. The next morning we told them (SAS) we had to have some clothes. They told us to go ahead and buy some at their expense, since they still had not located my bag. We spent that morning buying a warm, sweatshirt-type shirt, some underwear, socks, and sturdy shoes. Later I also bought a dress shirt, a sport coat, slacks, a warm sweater, and a suitcase. (My bags were not located for six days.) Although I appreciated the new clothes, I didn't need them and to this day they hang, rarely used, in our closet.

We flew to Alicante, Spain in about two weeks. After discussing it with the English skipper, we had decided this was about enough time for him to bring the boat from Crete to Alicante. When we landed in the airport at Alicante, another of the oh-so-clever gypsy thieves stole my newly replaced camera. I just turned my back on it for a few minutes while I talked to a travel agent. Advice? Never turn your back on your luggage anywhere in the Mediterranean countries.

We checked into a small hotel near the waterfront and awaited the appearance of Golden Bell at the customs quay. Daily we strolled the waterfront. During five days, we got to know each fence, gate, and post. We also, much to our pleasure, spent an evening in the local Plaza del Torros listening to a concert by a Balkan orchestra. We sat in the front row where we could almost touch the barricades behind which the clowns and picadores jump to escape the wrath of the bull. The music was excellent and well served the enchanting evening under the starry sky. We mused about the contrast between the normal use of the amphitheater and its use that night.

On the fifth day, we awoke to see the familiar twin masts of Golden Bell there at the customs quay. With anxious hearts we hurried over and greeted the crew who had just arisen, having entered port about midnight. The captain was over checking the boat and the people in at the customs office and soon returned. He asked us to please stay away until he had had a chance to clean up the boat. He made arrangements for the crew and himself to leave the next morning. We were so excited about having our beloved Golden Bell back that we slept restlessly that night and moved aboard the next day.

After a day of provisioning, we started down the coast of Spain. We enjoyed this part of the Spanish coast and put into a few quiet harbors. Our objective was the Cabo del Gato (Cape of the Cat) which, after we had rounded it, would put us into a new sea, the Alboran Sea, although for us it would still be the Mediterranean. We would also be entering a popular playground for Europeans with lots of beaches and marinas.

We rounded the cape, all right, but didn't have enough time to make the next harbor. "Let's just anchor off the beach," I suggested. The sea was calm and the beach promised good holding for the anchor. We were soon in place with the anchor down. We spent a quiet and restful night. It surprised us because it was one of the few times we have anchored anywhere except in a protected harbor, although we had seen numerous other boats doing it.

The next day we went on to a fine, new port called Almiramar. The Puerto Deportivo (sport port, rather than fishing port) was nearly empty which surprised us. But it was a long way from any population center and it was late in the year for the cruisers to be around. We left Golden Bell there for a couple of days while we went up to Granada in a rented car.

We visited the Alhambra, of course, that fabulous palace-fortress of the Moorish kings. It was built in the 13th and 14th centuries and by any standards is one of the world's most beautiful buildings.

The Moors came from Africa and attempted to found an Islamic empire, but conquered only half of the peninsula before the thrust ran out of steam. During their presence, they had a strong influence on the culture and architecture of Andalusia. They were finally driven out by King Ferdinand, after several years, in 1492. That was a good year! Perhaps the best-known legacy of the Moors is the lacy columns and intricate patterns of the Alhambra. The gardens were mystical. The halls and rooms were cool and airy. And the fountains danced with a sprightliness that soothed the soul. You may recall, if you're a fan of his, the charming small book written by Washington Irving, *Tales From Alhambra*. He stayed in one of the rooms in the Alhambra while writing it and other stories. Of course, today no one is allowed to stay there anymore, but it must have been a very mystical experience.

In Larnaca, Cyprus we had met a couple who had lived in Portland, retired, or should I say, "dropped out," bought a boat and with their two small children sailed around the world. Their boat Marinka was in the Almiramar marina, hauled out and stored and we had noticed it. They had said they were going to make a fast cruise to Spain and then fly back to the States for something to do with the children's education. Their very mature (mentally, not physically) 11-year-old daughter stood watches, both lookout and steering, and was as good a crew member as anyone could wish for. We saw them again in Gibraltar. They left for the Canary Islands a day earlier than we did. Marinka was a Westsail (a brand of boat) 42 and ours was a Westsail 32. The numbers refer to the length of the boat in feet.

We continued our leisurely pace along the Costa del Sol enjoying the tropical climate, hopping from marina to marina, or to be more correct, Puerto Deportivo to Puerto Deportivo. Some were surrounded by condominiums, but we didn't find that offensive. Some were not quite so developed, but all seemed to be a focal point of the villages.

I have mentioned the Spanish habit of strolling in the evening. Most of this strolling was done at the Puerto Deportivo and as a result, there were many cafes there. Have I mentioned that this stroll was a family affair? And that the end result was a meal, usually taken at about 9:00 p.m.. It was a very pleasant week or 10 days that we spent on the Costa del Sol. We could readily understand why it was a playground for the rich and famous.

    We approached Gibraltar with anticipation. Was it really going to look like the insurance logo? The guidebook told of currents and winds! Finally, out of the haze The Rock took shape and, yes, it did look like the logo. But from the east, there was a large white patch that was very curious. We finally guessed, and later confirmed, that it was a water catchment system. It makes sense, especially after Franco closed the border in 1969, claiming sovereignty. The British, of course, refused to acknowledge this and the border was re-opened in 1985—probably due to pressure from the many Spanish natives who worked there. The resident population is now about 50 percent Spanish, but England shows no sign of relinquishing control of this most strategic of positions, standing as it does at the very gate between the Atlantic and the Mediterranean.

    We rounded The Rock in a rather strong current and it seemed that we would never reach the Atlantic side and the marina. But repeated checks against the shore and the fact that we passed two ocean liners (at anchor) gave us encouragement. Finally we turned east and arrived off the breakwater. The marinas and small boat harbors are at the extreme east of the port just off the runway for the one landing strip that serves Gibraltar. The Rock is isolated from the hills to the east by a flat sandy plain that narrows to about 200 meters at the airport. The runway is, therefore, almost totally filled-in material which extends well out into the bay on either side of this strip. This makes a small harbor which is devoted almost entirely to pleasure boats.

Being anchored by the runway provided us with frequent entertainment. Whenever a plane took off, just before it revved up to full power, there was a large explosion near the end of the runway. This caused the cloud of seagulls to abandon this nice flat spot and fly away. Shortly thereafter, the plane took off. Shortly thereafter, the gulls returned. We examined the small (30 x 30 foot) platform and discovered a machine that apparently fires shotgun shells or something similar and automatically reloads for the next plane. The platform had no other discernable purpose.

We enjoyed Gibraltar. It was like no other place in the world. It is not just a big rock. It is miles of tunnels that honeycomb the rock to connect cannon ports, etc. The Rock contains, also, huge caverns and natural passages with magnificent stalagtites and stalagmites. An underground theater that seats hundreds is a natural cavern. Of course, we could not ignore the Barbary Apes, chimpanze-size monkeys that are, as far as anyone knows, the only known native European monkeys. The local "experts" in the guise of taxi-drivers, had varied opinions as to their origin. Some said that they were brought by sailors across the straits from Africa. Others said the limestone caverns that run through the rock continue on under the straits and up the other side to Africa and the monkeys used this route to gain The Rock. It is your choice. I take no position.

There were two groups of monkeys, according to our driver-expert. A tame group that sought the shelter and safety of the ranger's cages each night after panhandling the tourists all day. The others lived in the scrub near the top and are seldom seen.

Our crew from Portland arrived and we are now busily engaged in getting the boat ready for our crossing of the Atlantic. Reinhold Mahr has sailed with me many times and has made one crossing to Hawaii from Portland. Bob Carson was a sailor of long standing and both men were qualified navigators. We considered ourselves fortunate that these two men were willing to fly over and sail with us to the U.S. We planned to join a large group of cruisers in the Canary Islands and all leave at the same time. Last year there were two hundred in the group and this annual event includes lots of ceremonies, awards, and parties. We expect to have a wonderful time, and to be so busy in the Canaries that I won't have time to write again until the fleet arrives at the island of Barbados, which is just short of the Caribbean and in the western hemisphere.

Until then, keep well and happy.

Love,
  Paul & Emily

TRARCION FISHING HARBOR

17

Estepona,
Spain
December 21, 1988

Dear Friends,

In my last letter I said I would write you again from Barbados in the Caribbean. Well, I retract that statement as we have now gone to plan B. Plan A you recall was to cross the Atlantic taking Columbus' route via the Canaries with a large flotilla of other boats. This would have occurred except for one nasty little storm—but let's start at the beginning.

With Reinhold and Bob, our two crew for the

crossing, we soon got Golden Bell ready. We installed a wind generator to keep the batteries charged as we planned to use the ham radio and VHF a lot for communication with the other boats. And there was the SatNav, an electronic positioning device that uses satellites. This was not functioning properly, but when we tried to get it repaired, we discovered that it needed a new part that would take days and days to arrive. This we discovered on a Friday; we had planned to leave with the others on Sunday. At the local marine store, we could get a new one that would perform okay, so no problem. But, we had not reckoned with the administrative problems. The only ones available were in bonded stores. "So," I said, "Get one."

"It is not quite that simple," said the clerk. "It can only be released from the warehouse by the customs officials, and they only do it once a day. Then we deliver right after they release it, directly to your boat."

"Great, let's get it done," I replied.

The "Oh, I'm so terribly sorry" look returned to his face. He patiently explained, "This is Friday afternoon. They (customs) do not work on Saturday or Sunday, so the earliest we could get it to you would be Monday afternoon." We had hoped to leave with Marinka, friends we had first met in Cyprus, on Sunday. Oh well, we would only be a day behind them so I paid for the device and wished Marinka good sailing. Please remember, all four of us were qualified celestial navigators and both Reinhold and Bob were looking forward to practicing this art during the crossing. Why did I stubbornly insist on the SatNav? Because you get no sights on a cloudy day, while the SatNav delivers position sometimes every 10 or 15 minutes, although occasionally there is a gap of five hours between readings. I just like to cut the odds a little more in my favor. Loran, which we had used in the Med, was not available in Spain, nor would it be until we arrived in the States.

Monday finally came and we got our SatNav about 1300 (1:00 p.m.). I took me about 15 minutes to install it. We were cast off by 1330. The Great Adventure was about to begin! We had been watching some low pressure cells out about 100 miles off the straits but they had vanished on Saturday and were still conspicuously absent. These low pressure areas in that position cause a southwest wind— exactly in the direction we wanted to go and all cruisers avoid headwinds. They make for uncomfortable, slow going.

But this beautiful sunny afternoon caused us to leave in high spirits, although we had some concern about the heavy ship traffic in the straits. Our plan was to go almost to Point Tarif hugging the shore and then cut sharply across the ship traffic to the African (or Moroccan) side. It was a good strategy, and it worked, but it was a white-knuckle experience to see five freighters heading toward you from one direction and three from the opposite. Soon, we passed the light on Cape Spartel. It was dark by then and we decided to stay 100 miles off the African coast in the hopes of keeping out of the shipping lane that turned south. The chart we had indicated that the major shipping route was about 40 miles off the coast.

A mild breeze had sprung up so we shut off the engine and set all our sails. It was a fine, warm night, the kind that fill sailors' dreams. Watches were set and the ship settled into a routine. It was agreed that Emily would not stand night watches and that she would do the cabin chores.

Shortly after the sun rose, we trailed a line in the hope of having fresh tuna for the evening meal. Very soon, as I recall in about an hour, we had our fish. A fish in the water, however, is of little value. While we were attempting to land him into the boat, he shook off and vanished. A couple of hours later we had another one, and an hour after that, a third. Unfortunately, the results were the same.

We continued all that day to plow southwestward down the African Coast. During the morning, I talked to Marinka on the ham radio. We also set up a sort of net on the SSB, which you may remember is a long-distance system similar to the amateur bands. On this band, we had a daily rendezvous with another Portland boat and a German boat heading for the Madeira Islands and taking a different course than the one Columbus took. The Portland boat was Baba Wawa and the skipper was a member of our own yacht club in Portland. We had never met, but I thought it was unusual that three boats from the same modest city on the other side of the continent were, at the same moment, about 50 miles apart off the coast of Africa.

As the second day drew to a close, the wind strengthened a little and backed from northwest to west. It moved around to the southwest by morning and continued to gain strength. For reasons of comfort, and to avoid long tacks against the wind, we decided to heave-to and wait out the storm. We had a weather fax aboard and the morning transmission showed a rather strong low just about 100 miles off Gibraltar. Our old friend, The Nasty Low, was back. Oh well, we would just wait out the two or three days that it took for storms to dissipate or move on. Two days later, there was no change and the wind strength had increased to 45 knots. This is gale strength. The reason was apparent when the morning weather fax showed heavy isobar concentration up near Iceland. The low that was plaguing us had shifted 50 or 60 miles north, but was still basically in the same place—unmoving and just as deep.

To understand this better, as you look down on a low, in the northern hemisphere, the wind revolves around it in a counterclockwise direction. Since we were in the southeast quadrant that meant that the wind was blowing on our nose. Of course, we didn't need a chart to tell us this, but in a council of war, the wind being the enemy, we decided, since the low was moving north, to sail in a southerly direction as best we could and soon we would pass out of this cyclone. Great idea! By morning, with short sails, and the winds continuing to clock at 40 to 50 knots, our SatNav showed that we had moved about 20 miles west by north.

"Wrong tack," I said, so we changed to the starboard tack. By mid-afternoon, we had gained 20 miles almost due east. If we wanted to make some southing, we were obviously not going to do it by sailing. But, sailing gave us something to do and at least kept us from drifting downwind as we would have done while hove-to.

It was about day six of this storm that we encountered a Russian tanker. It was plowing through the 10 to 20 foot waves, right at us! I jumped onto the VHF and called them. No answer! I called again and again and activated our strobe light. No indication that they knew we were there. When this became apparent, I switched on the engine and, with full power, plowed at right angles to their course. They passed about 200 meters away from us, and it was then that we discovered they were Russian. I got on the VHF and chewed them out quoting all kinds of international regulations and stating my sincere promise to report them to Col-regs (an international body whose purpose is to prevent collisions at sea) as soon as I made the next port. No response. And you know, I don't think they ever knew that we were there. Kind of scary, and points out the need for a strict watch at sea.

That night on Bob's watch we got a 65-knot gust and a rolling wave at the same time and we got knocked down. "Knocked down" is the term sailors use when the boat is tipped so much that the mast hits the waters. The only thing worse is a roll-over in which the boat makes a complete roll. The knock-down occurred at night and Bob was on watch, but fortunately below. Golden Bell righted herself quickly and not too much water came in.

The next morning we had a meeting. This low was right in the same spot and showed no sign of weakening. Both Marinka and Baba Wawa were hove-to and getting tired. We were tired and a little scared after the knock-down. We took a vote.

Bob said, "I'd like to go back."

Emily said, "I'm tired and would like to go back."

Reinhold said, "Whatever you decide, I'll stick it out. It can't last forever."

So I said, "OK, let's set a course for wherever downwind will take us."

We turned downwind and set a couple of small sails. The change was dramatic. The ride of the boat smoothed, the wind reduced and the boat started ticking off the miles at near hull-speed. It is common for boats to "run" downwind in severe storms for just these reasons. There is only one problem and that is the risk of being "pooped." That's when a wave breaks just right and douses the deck with "green" or solid water. This happened not long after we turned and poor Bob was on deck. The water hits you with incredible force so that you get thoroughly soaked and, if you are not holding on tightly you can be swept along the deck and even off the boat. This is one of the reasons that on our boat, anyone on deck while we are at sea wears a safety harness and it must be snapped on. Bob changed into dry clothes and resumed his watch. Guess what happened about a half-hour later? Fortunately, he had one change of dry clothes left.

We decided to go into Cadiz on the west coast of Spain. Emily discovered that there was a new marina there at a place called Port Sherry. Was this the place that someone had told us about where they hand you a bottle of sherry when you register at the marina?

"We will find out," I said, "because that is where we are going."

We had an exhilarating sail downwind making six to seven knots all the way. Of course, Bob has the right to interject that it was not all exhilarating because of the two times he got doused with hundreds of gallons of the North Atlantic. But as a dry skipper, I had the right to respond with hearty cheerfulness, "It's all a part of sailing and you are now an old salt, right?"

It took us about 30 hours to fetch the Spanish coast and bay of Cadiz. We sailed into the large bay and, with some difficulty, located Port Sherry which we called on the VHF to announce our arrival and to request mooring. A very nice female voice responded with a delightfully seductive accent, "No problem." She then requested the usual information as to the length, beam, draft, etc. of our boat, and instructions about what to do when we entered the actual marina.

"OK," I said, "let's furl the sails and motor in the rest of the way." The crew jumped to respond to my orders. Except one. Emily asked, "Should we start the motor first?"

It started, ran long enough for us to get the sails down and then died. It refused to start again. So-o-o, up sails again. Now we would have to sail into the harbor and maneuver under sail there—a real test of the sailor's art. I had done it before, but never with this boat. I could do it again, I hoped. Just to be safe, I called the marina and told them that we had no motor and would they have a motorboat standing by to tow us in if the winds were adverse and the channel too narrow. We never needed it because when we were just outside the marina, we decided to give the motor one more chance. And it started!

Yes, the rumors had been correct. We were handed a bottle of sherry by the young woman at the marina office (she was as pretty as her voice) when we registered. This marina was also nearly empty and very new and modern. We were greeted by the small contingent of cruisers there who were waiting out the storm in order to start their crossing. On the ham radio that night, we talked with Marinka. They were still fighting the storm and growing increasingly desperate. Stan talked about reaching the end of his rope and going into Casablanca. This harbor had a very bad reputation. You needed an armed guard on your boat at all times to prevent thievery. He said that he would stick it out one more day.

The next day the low moved inland on Morocco and dissipated. Two boats left Port Sherry for the Canaries and motored nearly all the way. Marinka, ran out of fuel near the first of the Canary Islands and sat in a calm for a couple of days waiting for a breeze to take them in to the principal harbor of Las Palmas.

Bob expressed a strong desire to go home. He had had enough of the high seas for now. Emily was exhausted and was not enthusiastic about trying again. Reinhold was phlegmatic—whatever I wanted to do. Decision: we would cancel our plan to cross, sell Golden Bell in Spain and fly back to the States. This left me with an ache in my heart because I truly love long periods at sea, but not necessarily when they involve eight days of storm. I would miss the great crossing with the other boats and the fellowship that exists when you are with people who understand you. Each voyage is a challenge and I had met, but not beaten, this one. Perhaps it is this thing within me that keeps me, year after year, in this life. I don't know. But I do know that I felt a great sadness when Emily and I made this decision.

When we had cruised the Spanish coast just east of Gibraltar, we had spent a day or two in the pleasant harbor of Estepona, about 20 kilometers from Gib. There was a rather active yacht brokerage there and a small yard available for repairs and haul-out. We volunteered to take Bob to Malaga where he could get a plane for home. Then we would drive down to Estepona and see about selling Golden Bell. This motor trip would take us through the vineyards and up onto the plains (where the rain falls, mainly) of Andalusia and down to Malaga. We set out from Santa Marce, or Port Sherry, to Jerez, the principal town of the area. The Spanish pronunciation of the name sounds somewhat like Sherry. We traveled along the fertile coastal plains. At Jerez, we turned up the gentle slopes covered almost entirely with vineyards where they were growing the grapes from which the world-famous sherries and brandies were made.

Soon the hills became mountains and we wound our way up valleys that showed vestiges of an old stone road. They also contained cork oaks, some in orchards, some growing wild. We stopped to examine their bark. All mature trees had been stripped of their bark sometime in the past and many looked as though they would be ready in another year or two for a second harvest. Or third? Or tenth?

We continued on through some spectacular scenery to a village called Ronda. The distinguishing feature of Ronda is an awesome gulch that runs through the center of the city. It is 250 feet deep and has vertical sides. A two-lane stone bridge connects the two parts of the town and, I believe, is several hundred years old. It is also said that during the Spanish revolution, in the thirties, the communists marched intellectuals, such as doctors and teachers out onto the bridge and threw them off. It is not good to have people who think running loose in the perfect society. After an excellent meal in a restaurant on the town plaza, we drove across the bridge and down fertile valleys to the coast. From there we went to Tormalina where Bob would catch a taxi to the Malaga airport the next day.

Reinhold, Emily, and I then turned southwest and arrived at the Puerto Deportivo about 4:00 p.m. Yes, they could handle Golden Bell, yes they would advertise her in Britain (they were British expatriates). The harbormaster assured us that there would be a moorage for us when we arrived. Good! Now we headed back to Port Sherry and, after surviving a one-hour traffic jam in Algerciras (Gibraltar's satellite Spanish town), arrived home late in the evening.

To our cruising friends, we recommend Port Sherry as a launching point for an Atlantic crossing, or perhaps, a stop on the way to northern Europe. At the time we were there, repair facilities were not in place. But excellent facilities are contemplated. Coming from the Med, you can have your work done at Gibraltar where top-notch skills are available. But quit the noisy, exposed place quickly and take the one-day trip up to Cadiz Bay and Port Sherry. There you can relax and fine-tune the boat before you take off.

While you are there, please schedule a tour to a bodega. I emphasize "tour" because this gets you into one of the major wineries of the area. The one we visited bottled Harvey's Bristol Cream Sherry, a well-known dessert wine. We were conducted through the noisy bottling section and finally into the quiet of the cellar, which was the shed where the kegs of maturing wine were stored, row on row, three high. Each keg contained about 40 gallons and was dated.

An interesting feature in one of the cellars were the inscriptions in white chalk on the barrel-heads left there by former visitors. Bo Derek and Caroline Kennedy were a couple of the names that we saw. The prettiest lady in our group was invited to inscribe her name on a barrel. Incidentally, our guide did not speak English but he articulated his Spanish so clearly and slowly that even I was able to understand him.

After this, we were ushered out onto a sun-splashed

terrace where tables were set up. They held open bottles of the various wines produced by the company for our tasting pleasure. We were asked which of the wines we liked the most. Later, as we left, we were handed a bottle of our favorite.

After the tasting session, we were ushered down the street a couple of blocks to see the stable of Andalusian horses kept by the company. These magnificently beautiful and gentle animals were, quite probably, the highlight of Emily's visit to Andalusia, and perhaps all of Spain.

Now, more specifics about Plan B. After we sold Golden Bell on the European side of the Atlantic, we planned buy a new home on the U.S. side. Call us chicken if you wish, but two unusual storms that summer, not to mention the small ones, sort of convinced us that somebody up there didn't want us to cross the Atlantic. And, what was so infuriatingly unfair was that Sunchaser had never been in a storm of gale strength and she had sailed years longer and thousands of miles farther.

We are now busily engaged in cleaning, varnishing, painting, and packing and we hope to have Golden Bell in top shape for her new owner before we leave. That completed, we will cross the Atlantic, but by airplane and somewhat on schedule. We will search the east coast starting at Annapolis, the sailing center of the world, some say, and work down the coast to Florida searching for our new floating home. Somewhere in that sector is a boat that contains all that we want but still possesses the integrity of Golden Bell. Emily wants storage for more pots and pans and room to spread out her painting things. The old salt, me, wants a powerful engine and inside steering. We both want room for our guests to visit us and deck space for a quiet evening cocktail. We are also writing down possible names in case she is a new boat.

This is being written just before Christmas and our thoughts turn especially strongly at this season to our friends and family everywhere. A very heart-felt Felice Navidad and Nuevo Ano to you all. Our secretary says that we have lots of cards waiting to be forwarded to our next address. Isn't it wonderful to have friends?

    Love,
          Paul and Emily

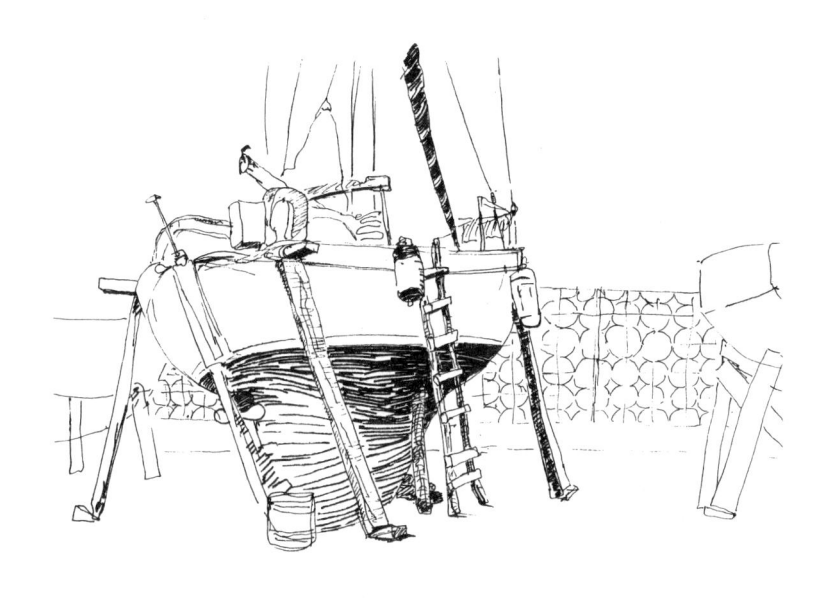

18

About Cruising and Solving Problems

Nearly everybody who stops to chat with us asks questions about boating life and what happens when unplanned things occur or sailing skills are taxed beyond their experience. "I suppose that we could have conjured up some dramatic, mystical answer, but acquiring the skills necessary to sustain yourself comfortably in the cruising lifestyle is just about the same as learning anything else. The same people who view our skills with awe have skills that they acquired by studious application of their own talents. One of my scientist friends, amazed that I had solved a difficult mechanical problem while she and Emily were out hiking, said "It must be the "Y" chromosome."

It does help to have had experience from childhood in solving mechanical and spatial problems, but I don't think this is something that is inherited. All right, I concede that it might be fifty percent chromosomal, but it is also fifty percent environmental. Note: the X-chromosome-endowed Tanya Abei is the youngest person of either sex, to sail around the world alone.

These are some of the questions people ask:

"Don't you get seasick?"

Only twice. This is a blessing that both Emily and I enjoy. If you have serious problems with this, pursue some other dream. However, we have friends who are seasick for about two days every time they make a passage. Then they get over it and enjoy. Pills and patches can help and many of our friends smooth over the rough spots with them.

"Do you fish a lot?"

No. When this lifestyle is your whole life, you don't need a diversion. You have a lot to do on the boat. And when you are in a harbor, you spend your time shopping or visiting the local museums, and trying to understand and enjoy the culture.

"How do you keep clean?"

You go outside when the rain falls and take a cake of soap. In ports, you try to find marinas that have shower and laundry facilities. At sea we used a "Sun Shower," a plastic bag which we laid on the deck until the sun warmed the two or three gallons in it. The bag was fitted with a small hose at the bottom and a nozzle. Both Emily and I could have a refreshing shower out of a three-gallon bag. Clothes can be washed in a bucket, and often are, using saltwater and detergent (Joy seems the best and is standard on all cruising boats) and rinsed by sacrificing a couple of gallons of fresh water. On long passages, we wore few clothes, if any, so laundry was not a big problem. While cruising in the more populated places our laundry demands became more important. Laundromats often were available, but if they weren't, there was always plenty of fresh water. We then hung the clothes on the life-lines. "Banners of domesticity," I called them.

"How about food and supplies? Can you find the things you want in far-away places?"

No. So you take what you can get. I went through a long peanut butter blackout but don't remember being hospitalized for it. In the Pacific, on all the settled islands, there is always a small general store. There are canned meats, mostly corned beef and tuna, canned vegetables and fruit, and there is always fresh bread. Unless you are expected, though, the baker on the island will bake only enough for the inhabitants. You can bake on a stove top, but a pressure cooker is helpful—no, almost essential. We ate very little fresh fish, as we seem to belong to that group of hapless people who can trail a line through a school of tuna and come up empty-handed. But many cruisers count heavily on their seafood to round out their larders and to avoid stretching the budget. All of the larger countries and heavily populated areas have a supermarket that often carries U.S. and European brands. Of course, you start the voyage well stocked in canned foods, dried foods, and other things that keep well. We did not have refrigeration on board until we bought our new boat "Elizabeth M" here in the States, but we found ourselves little handicapped by that lack.

"What do you do when you get sick or have an accident?"

You prepare as best you can. Emily was an M.D. so the skill was there if needed. We are thankful that it was never needed. But, skill is not enough. You need to prepare. We put together a medical kit containing what we thought a ship's medicine chest should contain. We included pain killers and even a pair of dental forceps and a surgical kit. We also took a couple of bottles of all-purpose vitamins. Ointments for sunburn and insect bites are a personal decision, not to be overlooked. I took CPR training and first-aid courses. There are several books written by doctors who sail, and seminars that address this problem. Another point to remember is that if you have long-range radio (ham or SSB), medical advice and assistance is not too far away.

Mosquito coils, roach powder, fly swatters and other weapons in the war with the insects are helpful—but be warned that you cannot win! Infestations of cockroaches are likely and can be minimized by never taking cardboard boxes on board and by dunking vegetables and fruit in seawater or washing them with a mild chlorine solution. This also will help keep down gastronomic invasions.

"Aren't you afraid of an accident while at sea or in some out-of-the-way place?"

Yes, but you do all that you can to eliminate the possibility. We never go on deck at sea without our safety harness on and clipped to a secure point on the boat by a short line. You soon learn the sailor's adage, "One hand for the work, one hand for the boat." We try to keep the decks as clear as possible of things that might cause one to trip. But safety is more a state of mind than anything. That means that in everything you do, you try to anticipate the worst that can happen and make sure that it doesn't.

"How do you keep yourself amused at sea, cooped up on a boat and all that?"

I am almost tempted to retort with the statement, "If you have to ask, you wouldn't understand." At sea the serenity is intoxicating and addictive. The waves are hypnotic. There is the same spirit there that exists when a group of people sit around a campfire at night and gaze wordlessly into it for long periods. The sea life is amazingly abundant and fun to watch. Turtles, sharks, shearwaters, albatrosses, schools of tuna and Mahi Mahi, whales, dolphins and flying fish are all there to entertain you. There is, of course, work on the boat, meals to prepare, reading, navigating, and knitting. There is a far-flung paperback exchange in place. At most of the stops, such as harbormasters' offices, taverns, and yacht clubs, there are shelves of paperbacks. You leave the ones you have read and take an equivalent stack of ones that you haven't. In well-populated anchorages, the cruisers organize a "trash and treasure" meet (called flea markets in the U.S.) where things such as paperbacks and unneeded boat equipment are purchased and traded.

"If no one knows for sure where you are, how can you get your mail?"

It is not as big a problem as one might think, but you have to be prepared to go long periods—weeks, even months without mail. You will have a rough idea of your schedule and route. Almost anywhere in the world, air mail shouldn't take more than two or three days to get there. Before you leave on your voyage, you change your address to that of someone you trust and who is not likely to move himself. You arrange for certain financial obligations to be taken care of. Your designated addressee holds all your mail until you contact him by telephone or airmail telling him where to ship the accumulation of your mail. We have had mail sent to harbormasters, port captains, marinas, general delivery, yacht clubs, American Express offices (which routinely do this sort of thing), and friends we have made along the way. For our addressee, we have used only two: my son and a secretarial service. Other cruisers have also used relatives, professional offices devoted to this service, yacht clubs, and sailing organizations. We recommend our present service, which is an office secretarial service, for several reasons. During working hours they are always there and answer the phone. Our son, bless his soul, travels a lot and the chances of us getting his answering machine is about five to one. The secretarial service sends our mail out UPS or Postal Air Express, or whatever way we want it within one or two hours after we call. They always have in stock all the packages, envelopes, etc. necessary to expedite the process. Furthermore, most of the letters in this book were first sent to them. They copied them and sent them out to our mailing list within one or two days. They also take telephone messages, put them in our box and we get them eventually. None of this is a burden on them! It is their business and they do it well—for only $12 per month.

    Long-distance telephoning is a problem for two reasons. First is the time difference that has to be computed in order to catch your recipient at home—you hope! "Let's see now, is Thursday his night for racquetball? Or is it Wednesday?" Second, the telephone systems in foreign countries are almost universally government owned. The number of instruments and outgoing lines is limited and they are of marginal quality. In Turkey, for example, getting an international call through is a matter of dialing steadily, sometimes for an hour or more, hoping that your signal will reach the international line just as someone hangs up. If you are an amateur radio operator, you can frequently, at the right time of day, catch a ham who has phone-patching equipment. A ham in Seattle talked at least weekly to his daughter in the South Pacific. We got most of our late-breaking news from home from her. Incidentally, it was magical almost, to go for months without political news from the States. Such serenity of mind!

"Did you carry enough fuel with you to cross the Pacific?"

Of course not. We had a sailboat and we sailed all the way. The motor was used only to get in and out of the harbors. We had enough fuel to cover about 700 miles, if necessary.

"How did you learn to sail? Have you sailed all your life? It must take a long time to get good enough to sail across an ocean."

It takes great skill to win competitive sailing races, but it does not take great skill to sail across an ocean. It is not much different from driving a car. Someone shows you how and you practice until you can make the boat go well. You read and study and practice raising, lowering, and trimming the sails. You soon learn that the boat goes faster if the sails are in certain positions, depending on which direction the wind is blowing. Some skippers are better sailors than others but we all get where we are going.

"How do you find your way when you can't see any land?"

We have several electronic devices and Emily and I are qualified celestial navigators. We learned the skills in classes at our local community college. The U.S. Coast Guard and your local power squadron offer free classes in the use of electronic devices and in coastal navigation. Coastal navigation is the process of sailing carefully near land. To do this, you need to learn to read charts.

The basic navigational instrument is the compass. It is almost essential that you have a steering vane. This is a device that steers your boat for you through an ingenious arrangement of ropes and a vane that senses the direction of the wind. When you sail long distances, you find the wind blows for long periods of time from the same direction so the steering vane keeps you continuously headed in the same direction. Using the ship's compass, you just set the steering vane to take you where you want to go. You must check it frequently, however, to make sure that the wind has not changed direction and that the vane, therefore, is not steering you in the wrong direction.

"Do you fix all those things that you have on the boat?"

Yes, a lot of them, but most of the problems are simple ones. You only need to know basically how they work but not all the details about them. For example, the depth sounder goes blank. At home, if the TV doesn't work, the first thing you do is see if the cord is plugged in. Because if the screen is blank, it probably isn't getting any electricity. Blown fuses, corroded terminals, and broken wires can do that to your depth sounder. Best advice is to always have a backup, as far as it is possible. If the depth sounder fails, we have a lead weight on a strong cord that we lower into the water to see how deep it is. We have several compasses, two or three radios, lots of spare ropes, a sewing machine, and lots of needles and heavy, waxed thread in case the sails need repairing. We carry extra pumps, a dinghy, and a life raft. These last two are in case the whole durn boat fails us! We have oil light in case the batteries get low and a solar panel to keep them from getting in that condition. We have two sextants in case we lose one overboard while taking a sight on a star. We have extra blocks and other tackle to replace the rigging if necessary. We have two stoves, one just a single burner that swings freely, for use in storms. Can we repair all these things? No. But we have spare parts for simple repairs, and backups so that we can get to the next port of call where we might find an experienced tradesman who can fix it.

"What if your motor quits?"

On a sailboat this is not the tragedy that it is on a motorboat. But, just to be safe, I enrolled in a course at our community college entitled, "Care and Feeding of Marine Diesel Engines." The chances are that such a course is not available to everyone everywhere but I suspect that it is offered frequently in sailing centers throughout the world. If not, pay a local diesel mechanic to come and go over your engine with you. Have him point out what you must do to keep it running and what are the most probable things that can go wrong. The rather bombastic instructor of our class said that 90 percent of the reasons an engine stops is because fuel is not getting to the injectors. After 12 years and 30,000 miles of cruising, I must say that he was right! I think it is important for me to say here that I would not put to sea in a boat with a gasoline engine. If you can't afford a diesel, my advice is to get a smaller boat with a diesel in it. Gasoline is a volatile fuel. I have seen boats burn to the waterline in minutes because the fuel ignited.

    And while we are on the subject of size, many people are amazed that we crossed the ocean in such a small boat. Size has little to do with a boat's seaworthiness. A cork floats as easily and safely as an ocean liner of steel. The design of the boat and its structural strength are the first characteristics to look for. I will not go into these factors as there are books written on the subject. In most cases, the weak link in the chain of survival is not the boat but the skipper and crew. That is why we never (well hardly ever) feel afraid on the high seas, even in a storm. Storms are annoying, but the boat can take it if properly handled.

    "But where do you get money? You can't take along a lot of cash and it seems foolish to have hundreds of $20 traveler's checks."

    Strangely enough, money was one of the least of our problems. Our solution may not be available to everyone, but it certainly worked smoothly. It all centers around the Visa charge card and a Cash Management Account with Merrill/Lynch, although I suspect that many other firms and banks offer similar conveniences. A debit account on your Visa is a must. With the Visa, you can get money in many banks around the world. In fact, we were never in a community of reasonable size where we could not walk in, present our Visa and walk out with cash in the local currency. If you have a debit account, when the slip from the overseas bank reaches your bank, the amount is deducted at the best available rate. If you do not have enough cash in the account, enough is borrowed from your investment account to cover it. When your mail finally catches up with you, you can write a check on your ordinary account and send it to your Cash Management account. This worked well for us. In addition, we had an American Express card and used it a few times to buy traveler's checks. We also needed it the two or three times that we received mail at the Amex office. We could also use it to cash checks of larger denominations if needed. We carried a couple thousand in traveler's checks and a few hundred in U.S. dollars. These were our emergency funds to be used in the unlikely event that we were jailed and had to pay a fine, to bribe officials, or in other emergencies of similar nature. U.S. currency speaks loudly all over the world. In Istanbul, Turkey, the taxi drivers would quote a price in Turkish lira, but accepted considerably less in U.S. dollars.

"Don't you have a lot of problems with languages, customs officials and things like that?"

Yes, of course, but this makes it all fun and interesting. Emily wants desperately to speak French fluently, so she did most of the talking in France. I profess some knowledge of Spanish so I did most of the talking in Spain. But, almost everywhere you will find that the people who deal with foreigners—waiters, customs officials, airport workers, taxi drivers—have made it their business to learn English. It does seem as though this is the unofficial language of the world. If people do not speak English, they seem to derive great pleasure in communicating in pictures and sign language. In Turkey, in a small village, our vehicle became mired in mud. I walked to the local constabulary and with pictures and signs and lots of smiles communicated our distress to the local officials. One of them went outside and came back in with a man. Through pictures, much laughing and nods of the head, I negotiated a fee for the services of his tractor. He followed me to the vehicle and with a mighty tug pulled us out. Everybody was happy—but neither of us understood a word that the other said.

Customs officials are another subject. They vary in devotion to duty, rigidity, and price throughout the world. We really only found one country where baksheesh was still prevalent—Turkey. In a couple of ports, there were flat charges for "paperwork" that were probably not in the customs manual. A suggestion is that you approach all customs and port officials with a reasonable amount in your pocket in local cash. Take it out while he or she is telling you how long it is going to take to get these papers stamped and toy with the cash. If their attitude changes, put your hand down on the desk with the cash in it. If your papers are signed, leave the cash on the desk, pick up the papers, and leave. Do not leave it unless you get what you want. It may be that what they are telling you is true. (Usually it isn't.) You must be surreptitious. There is no country where such behavior is legal.

"Aren't you worried about pirates, thieves and other dangers from the people in some of those backward countries?"

The answer is, yes. We minimized the problem of pirates by bypassing that part of the world where piracy is almost a legitimate profession. We did not go through the far east or the Indian Ocean. All of the places to be avoided are well known by yachtsmen. Firearms? Yes, we have them onboard, but most people agree that they are of dubious value. Every once in awhile I hear strange noises in the night as something goes "bump." It is comforting to me to have some protection aboard. I hope that I will never be faced with a situation where I will have to use it. A United States marshal said to me once, "Yes, I carry a piece, but my advice to you is not to bother unless you have been trained to kill and to shoot straight." Interesting thought. When checking into a country, firearms must be declared. So they turn out to be a bloody nuisance in the long run. To fail to declare them could put you in jail. My opinion, not shared by all cruisers, is that they are more trouble than they are worth.

And, finally, what is it that keeps us in this lifestyle year after year? No one has ever asked us why we love our lifestyle. If they did I have an answer. I think it is because both of us are romantics who are in a continuous search for freshness in our lives. Around the next bend of a river, across the next sea, on the next island there are new people to meet, new scenes to be seen, new history to be studied. Our minds and psyche absorb these experiences with an insatiable appetite and will continue to do so as long as we are physically able. Then, we will have a rich treasure of memories to recall and discuss for as long as we draw a breath. And then there is the host of friends all over the world to cherish and nurture. But most of all, there is the satisfaction that we have lived our dream and the self-assurance that goes with knowing we weren't too old to start living it.

*I have learned this at least
by my experiment:
That if one advances confidently
in the direction of his dreams,
and endeavors to live
the life which he has imagined,
he will meet with a success
unexpected in common hours.*

Henry David Thoreau

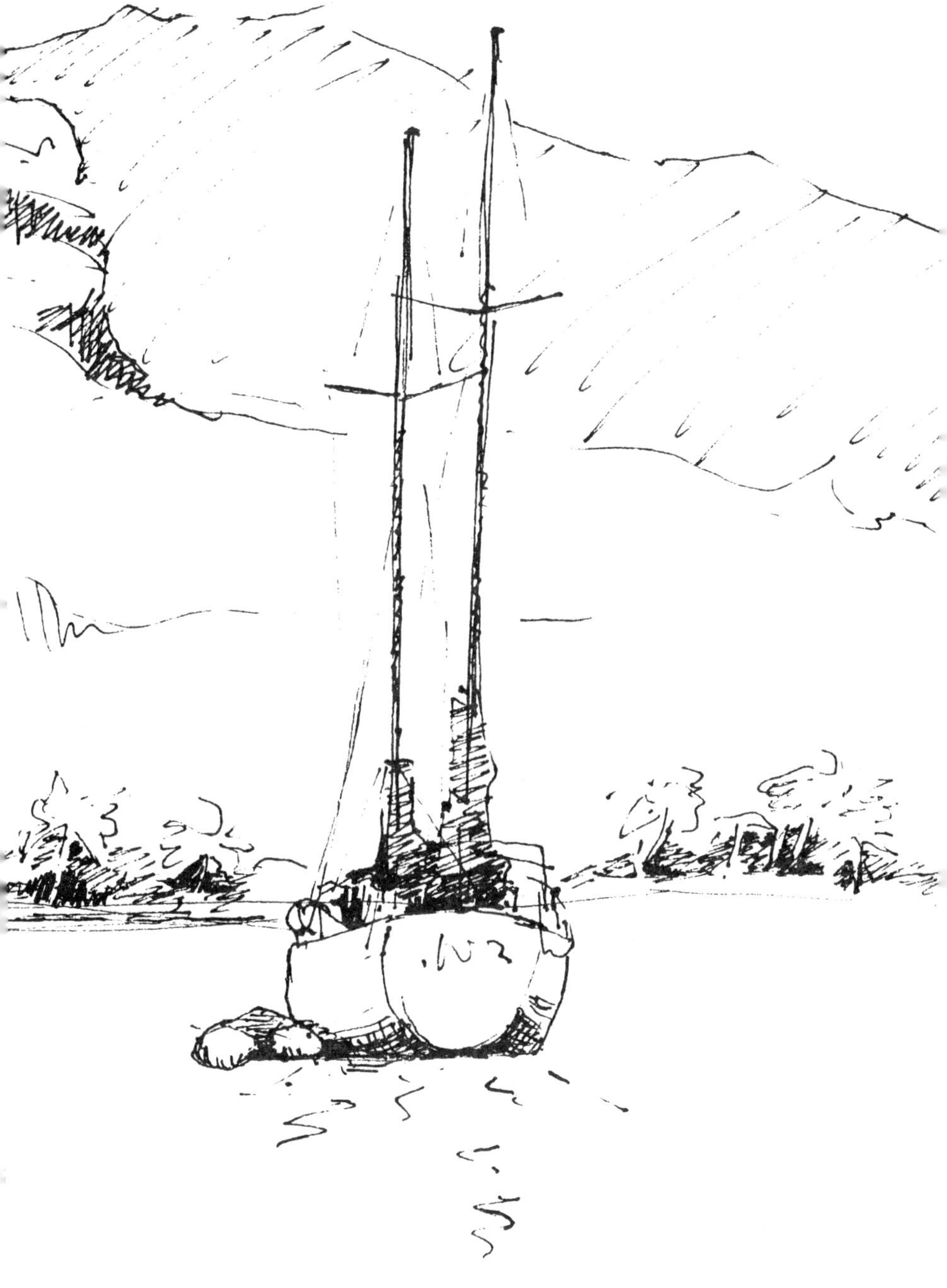